UX
MASTERY

The Art & Science of User Experience Design
Basics to Brilliance, 101 Strategies Explained

MAYUR CHAUDHARY
KISHORE KANKIPATI

Chennai • Bangalore

CLEVER FOX PUBLISHING
Chennai, India

Published by CLEVER FOX PUBLISHING 2024
Copyright © Mayur Chaudhary, Kishore Kankipati 2024

All Rights Reserved.

Paperback ISBN: 978-93-56489-86-8
Hardback ISBN: 978-93-56489-91-2

This book has been published with all reasonable efforts taken to make the material error-free after the consent of the author. No part of this book shall be used, reproduced in any manner whatsoever without written permission from the author, except in the case of brief quotations embodied in critical articles and reviews.

The Author of this book is solely responsible and liable for its content including but not limited to the views, representations, descriptions, statements, information, opinions and references ["Content"]. The Content of this book shall not constitute or be construed or deemed to reflect the opinion or expression of the Publisher or Editor. Neither the Publisher nor Editor endorse or approve the Content of this book or guarantee the reliability, accuracy or completeness of the Content published herein and do not make any representations or warranties of any kind, express or implied, including but not limited to the implied warranties of merchantability, fitness for a particular purpose. The Publisher and Editor shall not be liable whatsoever for any errors, omissions, whether such errors or omissions result from negligence, accident, or any other cause or claims for loss or damages of any kind, including without limitation, indirect or consequential loss or damage arising out of use, inability to use, or about the reliability, accuracy or sufficiency of the information contained in this book.

To My Pillars of Strength

To my parents, whose unwavering guidance and support have been my anchor; to my beloved partner and friend, and to our daughter, who fills my life with joy; to my brothers, extended family and to all my peers and industry professionals who knowingly and unknowingly made me a better version of yesterday.

Your presence in my life has been a true blessing, and I dedicate this book to each and every one of you with immense gratitude and love. Thank you.

Mayur Chaudhary

To My Navigators

This book is dedicated to my colleagues and friends, who have always been a source of inspiration and support. To my nephew Varun, whose curiosity and enthusiasm motivate me to keep learning and growing. To my family, whose unwavering love and encouragement have been my foundation. And to my beloved Swami, Bhagawan Sri Sathya Sai Baba, whose divine guidance and teachings have continuously steered my life in the right direction. Your influence and support have made this journey possible.

Kishore Kankipati

About Mayur Chaudhary

Born in Bihar, India, curiosity has always been my guiding star. I developed a deep passion for making a difference and getting out of my comfort zone, which led me to a fulfilling career in UX design and research spanning over 25 years.

My journey has traversed diverse industries, including e-commerce, fintech, hospitality, retail, automotive, real estate, consulting and others. Collaborating with renowned companies such as Microsoft, Accenture, Cisco, SAP, OLX, Myntra (Flipkart), Magicbricks, and more has been a privilege. These experiences have endowed me with invaluable insights and the expertise to craft user experiences that drive business success.

My passion extends beyond design. With an intention to give back to the professional community, I founded RethinkingUX, India's largest design community and a thriving global hub for learning, growth, and collaboration. As founder and advisor, I am dedicated to empowering aspiring UX designers, researchers, and product makers to unlock their full potential and shape the future of the industry.

I firmly believe that "every problem has a design solution," and I encourage everyone to be human centric, data informed in their execution and above all a continued learner.

About Kishore Kankipati

Kishore Kankipati, a dedicated UX designer since 2014, has significantly contributed to various projects across industries and geographies.

A self-taught expert, he has honed his skills through short training programs. Kishore's professional milestones include the Dynamics 365 web client refresh for Microsoft and user-centric solutions at Philips, particularly in oncology, streamlining doctors' workflows, and expediting patient diagnoses.

His excellence in design has earned him prestigious awards like the Red Dot and iF Design Awards.

With a Master's degree in Computer Applications, his career began in 2001 as a faculty trainer and later as an accountant. Kishore pledges to produce impactful, human-centric designs in the spirit of Bhagawan Sri Sathya Sai Baba's teachings.

In his free time, he explores design trends and stays updated with the latest in technology.

Introduction

Welcome to "UX Mastery: The Art & Science of User Experience Design." Basics to Brilliance, 101 Plus Strategies Explained.

A comprehensive guide designed to elevate your understanding and practice of user experience (UX) design. Whether you are a seasoned UX professional, a product manager, or someone new to the field, this book aims to provide you with the tools, techniques, and insights needed to create exceptional user experiences.

In today's digital age, the user experience is more critical than ever. It is the bridge between technology and the people who use it. A well-crafted UX can transform a product from merely functional to delightful, from confusing to intuitive, and from forgettable to indispensable. This book is the culmination of Mayur Chaudhary's 25+ years of experience in UX design and research, distilled into actionable insights and practical techniques that you can apply to your projects.

Throughout this book, you will discover a blend of art and science in UX design. The art lies in understanding human emotions, behaviours, and aesthetics, while the science involves data-driven decision-making, usability principles, and systematic processes. Together, they form the foundation of mastery in UX design.

As you embark on this journey, you will explore 101 plus industry techniques that will shine a light on your product design processes.

Each technique is presented with practical tips, real-world examples, and step-by-step applications to help you integrate them into your workflow seamlessly.

Thank you for choosing "UX Mastery: The Art & Science of User Experience Design." Let's begin this exciting journey towards creating user experiences that not only meet but exceed user expectations.

"Tools are just a medium; it's the mindset that matters."
- **Mayur Chaudhary**

How To Use This Book

This book is crafted to be a go-to resource for both novice and seasoned UX professionals & product managers, offering actionable insights and detailed methodologies to enhance your design processes.

Step-by-Step Guidance

- **Follow the Phases:** The book is structured around key phases of the UX design process - Discover and Empathize, Synthesize and Strategize, Conceptualize and Innovate, and Envision and Embody. Each section provides in-depth techniques and tools specific to that phase.

- **Apply Techniques:** Use the detailed instructions and tips provided for each technique to apply it to your projects.. Whether it's conducting Contextual Inquiries or creating High-Fidelity Prototypes, follow the outlined steps to ensure thorough and effective execution.

- **Integrate with Teams:** The book emphasizes collaboration. Engage your team in the methods discussed, leveraging collective insights and fostering a user-centered design culture.

- **Iterate and Refine:** UX design is iterative. Use this book to continually refine your approach based on user feedback and evolving project needs.

Who Should Read This Book?

This book is designed for a wide range of professionals involved in creating user experiences, including:

- **UX Designers:** Whether you are just starting out or have years of experience, this book provides valuable insights and advanced techniques to enhance your design skills.

- **Product Managers:** Gain a deeper understanding of user-centered design principles to better align product features with user needs.

- **Developers:** Understand the design thinking process and how to collaborate effectively with designers to create seamless user experiences.

- **Researchers:** Learn detailed methodologies for gathering and analyzing user data to inform design decisions.

- **Business Stakeholders:** Understand the importance of UX in achieving business goals and how to support UX initiatives within your organization.

What's In This Book?

This book is a comprehensive resource that covers a wide array of topics and techniques essential for successful UX design:

- **Discover and Empathize:** Techniques like Contextual Inquiry, Diary Studies, Ethnographic Studies, and User Interviews to deeply understand user needs and behaviors.

- **Synthesize and Strategize:** Methods for organizing insights and defining strategic direction, including Affinity Mapping, Task Analysis, and SWOT Analysis.

- **Conceptualize and Innovate:** Creative techniques for ideation and problem-solving, such as Brainstorming, Concept Mapping, and Storyboarding.

- **Envision and Embody:** Practical guidance on prototyping and visual design, covering Rapid Prototyping, Paper Prototyping, Interactive Wireframes, and more.

- **Orchestrate and Align:** Strategies for effective project and stakeholder management, including Risk Analysis, ROI of UX Design, and Design Sprints to ensure cohesive team alignment and project success.

- **Craft and Build:** Detailed approaches to developing high-quality user interfaces, including Component Libraries, Design Systems, and Front-End Development best practices to ensure consistency and usability.

- **Test and Validate:** Robust methods for testing and validating designs, such as Usability Testing, A/B Testing, and Accessibility Audits to ensure the design meets user needs and standards.

- **Launch and Monitor:** Guidelines for successfully launching and monitoring products, including Go-To-Market Strategies, Analytics Setup, and User Feedback Loops to ensure continuous improvement.

- **Evolve and Scale:** Techniques for scaling and evolving UX practices, including Design Ops, Continuous Improvement Processes, and Scaling Design Systems to maintain design quality and efficiency as the product grows.

What Comes With This Book?

Alongside the rich content, this book includes several supportive elements to enhance your learning and application of UX principles:

- **Case Studies**: Real-world examples from companies that illustrate the application of various UX techniques and their outcomes

- **Tips and Best Practices:** Expert advice and tips to ensure you get the most out of each technique and avoid common pitfalls.

- **UX Design Blueprints:** A collection of method diagrams and templates that serve as blueprints for applying UX techniques throughout the product development process. Adapt these blueprints to suit your specific needs and streamline your UX design process.

- **Additional Resources:** Recommendations for further reading, online courses, and communities to continue your learning journey in UX design.

This book is a thorough guide designed to be both a reference and a practical manual. With the inclusion of UX templates, you'll have a hands-on resource to help you apply the techniques and methodologies covered in the book, streamlining your UX design process and enhancing your overall effectiveness as a UX practitioner.

★ All company names and trademarks mentioned in this book are the property of their respective owners and are used for illustrative and information purposes only.

Contents

XIV Quick Reads on UX Foundations

1 Discover and Empathize

2   Contextual Inquiry
4   Diary Studies
6   Ethnographic Studies
8   User Interviews
10 Empathy Mapping
12 Persona Creation
14 Stakeholder Interviews
16 User Journey Mapping
18 SWOT Analysis
20 Competitive Analysis

23 Synthesize and Strategize

24 Affinity Mapping
26 Task Analysis
28 Jobs To Be Done
30 Value Proposition Design
32 Business Model Canvas
34 Feature Matrix
36 Gap Analysis
38 Kano Model
40 MoSCoW Method
42 Requirement Prioritization

45 Conceptualize and Innovate

46 Brainstorming
48 Concept Mapping
50 Mind Mapping
52 Sketching
54 Storyboarding
56 Scenario Development
58 Six Thinking Hats
60 Design Thinking
62 Lean UX
64 Service Design
66 Participatory Design

69 Envision and Embody

70 Rapid Prototyping
72 Paper Prototyping
74 Low-fidelity Prototyping
76 Interactive Wireframes
78 High-fidelity Prototyping
80 Clickable Prototypes
82 Visual Language & Brand Study
84 Animation Timing
86 Color Theory
88 Design Tokens
90 Grid Systems
92 Iconography

XI

94	Micro-interactions	150	Pair Designing
96	Mood Boards	152	User Acceptance Testing (UAT)
98	Style Guide Development	154	Version Control
100	Typography Studies	156	Design Handoff
102	Visual Hierarchy	158	Component Library
104	Design System	160	QA Testing

107 Evaluate and Refine

108	Usability Testing
110	A/B Testing
112	Guerrilla Testing
114	Wizard of Oz Testing
116	Responsive Design Testing
118	Heuristic Evaluation
120	Cognitive Walkthrough
122	Usability Checklist
124	In-person Observations
126	Remote Usability Tests
128	Eye Tracking
130	Heatmaps
132	Analytics Monitoring
134	Customer Satisfaction Score
136	Net Promoter Score
138	System Usability Scale
140	Time-on-task Measurement
142	Error Rate Measurement

145 Execute and Launch

| 146 | Agile Development |
| 148 | DevOps Pipeline Integration |

163 Analyze and Enhance

164	AI-led Personalized Experiences
166	Predictive User Feedback
168	Churn Rate Analysis
170	Cohort Analysis
172	Conversion Funnel Analysis
174	Feedback Surveys
176	Field Survey
178	Iterative Testing
180	Lifetime Value Analysis
182	Longitudinal Study
184	Performance Metrics
186	User Analytics

189 Evolve and Expand

190	Design for Scalability
192	Design for Security
194	Scalability Testing
196	Design for Performance
198	Design for Accessibility
200	Design for Inclusivity
202	Design for User Engagement
204	Design for User Retention

206 Design for User Acquisition
208 Design for User Onboarding
210 Design for User Feedback
212 Gamification

215 Orchestrate and Align

216 Project Management
218 Stakeholder Management
220 Risk Analysis
222 ROI of UX Design
224 Negotiation Skills
226 Design Reviews
228 Design Sprints

231 UX Design Blueprints

232 Contextual Inquiry
233 Ethnographic Studies
234 User Interviews
235 Persona Creation
236 User Journey Mapping
237 Competitive Analysis
238 Affinity Mapping
239 Task Analysis
240 Jobs To Be Done
241 Value Proposition Design
242 Business Model Canvas
243 Brainstorming
244 Lean UX
245 System Usability Scale
246 Time on Task Measurement
247 Component Library
248 Concept Mapping
249 Scenario Development
250 Rapid Prototyping
251 Usability Testing
252 A/B Testing

253 References
255 Index

Quick Reads on UX Foundations

Before diving into the core techniques and methods of UX design, it's essential to establish a solid foundation. This section provides a curated selection of quick reads that will help you grasp the fundamental concepts and principles of User Experience.

The Importance of UX in Product Design and Management

User Experience (UX) design is no longer a luxury; it is a necessity. In an increasingly competitive market, the success of a product often hinges on the quality of its user experience. But what exactly makes UX so crucial in product design and management?

1. **Enhancing User Satisfaction:** At its core, UX design is about understanding and meeting the needs of users. A product that is easy to use, intuitive, and enjoyable can significantly enhance user satisfaction. Satisfied users are more likely to become loyal customers, recommend the product to others, and provide positive reviews.

2. **Driving Business Success:** Good UX design can directly impact a company's bottom line. By improving usability and accessibility, companies can reduce customer support costs, increase conversion rates, and boost customer retention. A well-designed product can differentiate a company from its competitors, creating a unique value proposition that attracts and retains customers.

3. **Reducing Development Costs:** Investing in UX design early in the product development process can save time

and money in the long run. By identifying and addressing usability issues before the product is launched, companies can avoid costly redesigns and rework. This proactive approach leads to a more efficient development process and a higher-quality final product.

4. **Facilitating Innovation:** UX design encourages a user-centered approach to innovation. By focusing on the needs and behaviors of users, companies can identify new opportunities for innovation and create products that truly resonate with their target audience. This user-centered mindset fosters creativity and drives the development of groundbreaking solutions.

5. **Building Brand Loyalty:** A positive user experience can significantly enhance brand perception and loyalty. When users have a seamless and enjoyable experience with a product, they are more likely to develop a strong emotional connection with the brand. This connection translates into long-term loyalty and advocacy, which are invaluable assets for any company.

6. **Informing Product Strategy:** UX research provides valuable insights into user behaviors, preferences, and pain points. These insights can inform product strategy, helping companies make data-driven decisions that align with user needs and market trends. By integrating UX research into the product development process, companies can create products that are not only functional but also highly relevant and desirable.

Discover and Empathize

This phase focuses on deep user understanding, uncovering insights, and building empathy through immersive research techniques.

1. Contextual Inquiry
2. Diary Studies
3. Ethnographic Studies
4. User Interviews
5. Empathy Mapping
6. Persona Creation
7. Stakeholder Interviews
8. User Journey Mapping
9. SWOT Analysis
10. Competitive Analysis

Discover and Empathize

Contextual Inquiry

How might we

Deeply immerse ourselves in users' environments, observing their genuine interactions, challenges, and workflows.

What you can do with the method...

Contextual inquiry offers a front-row seat to users' genuine interactions in their natural habitats. This method provides nuanced insights, unearthing real-world challenges, barriers, and opportunities. By observing tasks in context, designers can grasp the full scope of the user experience, including external factors that might impact product interactions.

Tip

Adopt a learner's mindset, allowing users to be the teachers. As you observe, resist the urge to jump in or correct. Focus on understanding their perspective, not on the solution. Your primary role is to gather insights; solutions come later. Nuanced questions can reveal deeper motivations, but timing is key.

 Contextual inquiry can uncover 30% more usability issues compared to traditional user interviews. (Source: Nielsen Norman Group)

Discover and Empathize

Contextual Inquiry

How the method is applied

1. **Objective Setting:** Clearly define what you aim to understand from this inquiry. Is it a specific task, behavior, or broader user context?

2. **Participant Selection:** Choose a diverse mix of users to ensure varied perspectives and insights.

3. **In-the-Field Observation:** Immerse in the user's environment, taking detailed notes of behaviors, interactions, and external factors.

4. **Intermittent Engagement:** While primary focus is on observation, engage occasionally to ask clarifying questions or delve deeper into observed behaviors.

5. **Data Collation:** Post-session, organize your notes, recordings, and any photographs. This becomes the foundation for analysis.

6. **Insight Extraction:** Review data to identify patterns, pain points, and opportunities. These insights will guide subsequent design decisions.

 IDEO and many other organisations conducts contextual inquiries to understand how users interact with products in their natural environments.

3

Discover and Empathize

Diary Studies

How might we

Understand users' behaviors, feelings, and interactions over a period of time in their natural environment.

What you can do with the method...

Diary Studies empower users to document their interactions, emotions, and challenges over time, offering a longitudinal view of their experiences. Participants maintain diaries, logging specific events, tasks, or feelings related to the product or service in focus. This method captures evolving behaviors, daily routines, and situational contexts, providing richer, temporally-spread insights compared to one-time research methods.

Tip

Consistency is key. Encourage participants to make regular entries and ensure they understand the importance of detailed, genuine reflections. A prompt or reminder can be beneficial in maintaining consistent logs throughout the study duration.

 Diary studies can provide 40% more insights into user behavior over time compared to single-session studies. (Source: User Experience Magazine)

Diary Studies

How the method is applied

1. **Determine Study Goals:** Define the specific interactions, behaviors, or experiences you wish to capture over time.

2. **Select Participants:** Choose users that represent diverse personas, ensuring varied perspectives in the study.

3. **Provide Diaries & Instructions:** Equip participants with diaries or digital logging tools. Offer clear guidelines on what and how to document.

4. **Set Duration & Check-ins:** Decide on the study's length. Schedule regular check-ins or reminders to keep participants engaged and consistent.

5. **Collect & Review Entries:** At study's end, gather all diaries/logs. Review entries, looking for patterns, commonalities, or unique insights.

6. **Analyze & Report:** Synthesize the collected data, identifying key themes, behaviors, and feedback. Translate these findings into actionable design recommendations.

 Fitbit uses diary studies to gain insights into users' daily habits and how their products fit into their lives.

Ethnographic Studies

How might we

Immerse in users' natural settings, capturing authentic behaviors, motivations, and challenges.

What you can do with the method...

Ethnographic Studies delve into users' natural environments, offering a firsthand view of behaviors and interactions. By immersing yourself in their world, you grasp cultural norms, routines, and genuine challenges. It transcends traditional research, capturing raw insights as you live the user experience. This method reveals unspoken dynamics and environmental factors that impact interactions with products or services.

Tip

Always be a passive observer in ethnography. Your role is to blend into the environment, capturing genuine behaviors without influencing them. Take comprehensive notes, but also absorb the ambiance, culture, and unspoken dynamics. Authenticity is the key; the deeper your immersion, the richer the insights.

 Ethnographic studies can increase user empathy and understanding by 60%, leading to more user-centered designs. (Source: Design Council)

Discover and Empathize

Ethnographic Studies

How the method is applied

1. **Define Objectives:** Target specific behaviors, routines, or cultural norms for observation.

2. **Select Sites & Prepare:** Pick environments like homes or workplaces aligning with study aims. Equip with tools—notebooks, cameras, recorders and familiarize yourself with the community.

3. **Observe & Immerse:** Dedicate time to the user's environment. Join in activities for genuine insights, ensuring you don't skew outcomes.

4. **Engage Informally:** Mainly observe, but sporadic interactions or brief chats can deepen understanding of observed behaviors.

5. **Document Observations:** Consistently record detailed notes, highlighting particular interactions, nuances, and remarkable moments.

6. **Analyze & Conclude:** After the study, review findings, pinpointing patterns and distinct insights. Draft a comprehensive report spotlighting primary discoveries and design suggestions.

 Intel conducts ethnographic studies to understand how technology is used in different cultures and contexts.

Discover and Empathize

User Interviews

How might we

Gather deep insights directly from users about their experiences, needs, and challenges.

What you can do with the method...

User Interviews serve as a direct channel to the user's mind and emotions. By engaging users in one-on-one conversations, you dive deep into their experiences, understanding their pain points, motivations, and aspirations. This qualitative method shines in revealing the "why" behind user behaviors. Whether it's for initial exploratory research or later-stage validation, these interviews are invaluable in crafting user-centric designs.

Tip

Every interaction has a story behind it. Utilize techniques like the "Five Whys" to uncover deeper motivations and root causes behind user behaviors. Always maintain a neutral stance, allowing users to freely express their experiences. Dive deep, but ensure you're guiding without leading, capturing genuine insights.

 User interviews can provide 70% more qualitative insights compared to surveys alone. (Source: UserTesting)

User Interviews

How the method is applied

1. **Define Research Goals:** Identify the core questions and insights you're aiming to extract from participants.

2. **Draft an Interview Guide:** Structure a set of questions and topics to ensure consistency across sessions.

3. **Recruit Participants:** Target users that represent your user personas, ensuring a diverse mix for comprehensive insights.

4. **Conduct the Interviews:** Engage users in conversations, balancing structured questions with open-ended discussions to capture spontaneous insights.

5. **Document Responses:** Transcribe or note down responses in real-time. Audio or video recordings can be valuable for revisiting nuances.

6. **Analyze & Synthesize:** Post-interview, review all data, identifying patterns, recurring themes, and unique insights. Translate these into actionable design recommendations.

 OLX conducts user interviews to gather feedback and insights to inform product improvements and new features.

Discover and Empathize

Empathy Mapping

How might we

Understand and visualize the user's experiences, emotions, and motivations to inform and improve the design process.

What you can do with the method...

Empathy mapping involves creating a visual representation of what users say, think, do, and feel. It helps you step into the user's shoes and understand their needs, pain points, and desires. By doing so, you can design solutions that are more aligned with user expectations and create more engaging and effective experiences.

Tip

Involve team members from diverse backgrounds and disciplines to create a more comprehensive and well-rounded empathy map.

 Teams that use empathy mapping experience a 40% increase in customer satisfaction (IDEO U)

Empathy Mapping

How the method is applied

1. **Define User Segments:** Identify the key user segments or personas to create empathy maps for.

2. **Gather User Insights:** Collect data on users' behaviors, thoughts, feelings, and motivations through research, interviews, and observations.

3. **Categorize Insights:** Organize user insights into four quadrants: Says, Thinks, Does, and Feels.

4. **Identify Pain Points and Opportunities:** Analyze the empathy map to uncover user pain points, needs, and opportunities for design.

5. **Share and Apply Insights:** Share the empathy map with the team and use the insights to guide design decisions and prioritize features.

 The design team at a financial services company used empathy mapping to understand the needs and challenges of millennial investors. By uncovering key insights, such as their desire for simple, mobile-first experiences, the team was able to create a more engaging and user-centered investment platform.

Discover and Empathize

Persona Creation

How might we

Understand the behavior, goals, needs, and limitations of our diverse user base to inform and guide the design process, making it user-centered and data-driven.

What you can do with the method...

Contextual inquiry offers a front-row seat to users' genuine interactions in their natural habitats. This method provides nuanced insights, unearthing real-world challenges, barriers, and opportunities. By observing tasks in context, designers can grasp the full scope of the user experience, including external factors that might impact product interactions.

Tip

Persona Creation is a method that synthesizes research into user archetypes. This helps teams empathize with end-users and make informed design decisions. Personas capture essential qualities of large user segments, helping to predict how they might interact with a product or service.

 Using personas can make design teams 2.5 times more effective at creating user-centered products. (Source: Nielsen Norman Group)

Persona Creation

How the method is applied

1. **Compile Research:** Gather user data from interviews, surveys, analytics, and market research to form a foundation for your personas.

2. **Analyze & Synthesize:** Identify common behavioral patterns, goals, skills, and needs that emerge from your data.

3. **Craft Personas:** Develop personas with names, photos, and narratives that encapsulate the essence of your user segments.

4. **Detail Scenarios:** Include scenarios that show how the personas interact with your product or service in their daily lives.

5. **Apply to Design:** Use personas as references throughout the design process to ensure decisions meet real user needs.

6. **Review & Refine:** Continuously update personas with new insights from ongoing research to keep them relevant and accurate.

 Spotify, Netflix, Myntra, and other organisations create user personas to guide product development and ensure features align with user needs and preferences.

Discover and Empathize

Stakeholder Interviews

How might we

Gather insights from project stakeholders, understanding their perspectives, goals, and concerns.

What you can do with the method...

Stakeholder Interviews are structured conversations with individuals who have a vested interest in the project's outcome. They can be team members, executives, clients, or even external partners. These interviews shed light on the stakeholders' visions, expectations, potential roadblocks, and success metrics. By engaging with stakeholders, designers can align project goals, prioritize features, and foresee challenges, ensuring a more holistic and supported design process.

Tip

Active listening is key. While it's essential to ask the right questions, equally vital is genuinely hearing and understanding stakeholder feedback. Their insights often extend beyond design, touching on business strategy, market dynamics, or organizational challenges.

 Stakeholder interviews can uncover 40% more project requirements and constraints compared to document analysis alone. (Source: Project Management Institute)

Stakeholder Interviews

How the method is applied

1. **Identify Stakeholders:** Determine individuals with crucial influence or stakes in the project's success, from team members to external partners.

2. **Draft Interview Guide:** Create a list of probing questions to unearth their goals, apprehensions, and expectations related to the project.

3. **Coordinate Sessions:** Set up interview timings, ensuring an environment conducive to open dialogue and undistracted conversation.

4. **Engage & Document:** Conduct interviews, emphasizing active listening. Simultaneously, note critical points, insights, or potential challenges shared.

5. **Analyze Collective Feedback:** Post all interviews, collate and review feedback to spot recurring themes, unique insights, and areas of alignment or contention.

6. **Strategize Design Direction:** Use the synthesized insights to influence design decisions, ensuring alignment with stakeholder vision and addressing raised concerns.

 GE conducts stakeholder interviews to align product development with the needs and goals of key stakeholders.

User Journey Mapping

How might we

Visualize a user's experience, understanding interactions and emotions across touchpoints.

What you can do with the method...

User Journey Mapping is a visualization technique that chronicles a user's experience with a product or service, from initial contact to final interaction and beyond. It highlights users' feelings, motivations, and questions for each touchpoint, revealing opportunities and pain points. By mapping out these journeys, designers and stakeholders gain a holistic view of the user experience, facilitating informed decisions that enhance user satisfaction and drive conversions.

Tip

Remember, journeys can vary based on user personas. It's beneficial to create multiple maps catering to different user profiles to capture a broad spectrum of experiences.

 User journey mapping can improve the user experience by 30% by identifying pain points and opportunities for enhancement. (Source: Forrester)

User Journey Mapping

How the method is applied

1. **Define Objectives:** Understand what you aim to achieve with the map, be it improving a process or enhancing user satisfaction.

2. **Identify Personas:** Determine the key user profiles that will be the focus of the journey map.

3. **List Touchpoints:** Enumerate all interaction points a user has with your product or service.

4. **Map the Journey:** For each persona, chart out the steps they take, from awareness to loyalty, documenting their actions, thoughts, and feelings at each touchpoint.

5. **Highlight Pain Points:** Mark areas where users experience friction, confusion, or dissatisfaction. These are opportunities for improvement.

6. **Collaborate & Refine:** Share the map with stakeholders and team members, gathering feedback. Iteratively refine the map, ensuring it remains a dynamic tool that evolves with user needs and business goals.

 Starbucks uses user journey mapping to understand and optimize the customer experience across all touchpoints.

Discover and Empathize

SWOT Analysis

How might we

Assess internal and external factors influencing a product's success and potential challenges.

What you can do with the method...

SWOT Analysis is a strategic tool that evaluates a product's Strengths, Weaknesses, Opportunities, and Threats. By analyzing internal factors (strengths and weaknesses) and external factors (opportunities and threats), it provides a comprehensive overview of a product's current standing and future potential. This framework aids in identifying areas of advantage, potential pitfalls, and external factors that might impact product success or vulnerability.

Tip

While SWOT is a powerful tool, it's crucial to be objective and honest in your assessment. Avoid confirmation biases. Engaging a diverse team or stakeholders can offer varied perspectives, ensuring a more rounded analysis.

 70% of companies use SWOT analysis as a strategic planning tool to identify strengths, weaknesses, opportunities, and threats. (Source: Harvard Business Review)

SWOT Analysis

How the method is applied

1. **Define Objective:** Clearly articulate what you aim to achieve with the SWOT Analysis, be it product evaluation, strategy formulation, or competition assessment.

2. **List Strengths:** Identify internal positive attributes, resources, or capabilities that give the product an edge.

3. **Pinpoint Weaknesses:** Recognize internal limitations, areas of improvement, or factors causing competitive disadvantage.

4. **Spot Opportunities:** Look externally to find conditions, trends, or changes that the product can leverage for growth or advantage.

5. **Identify Threats:** Examine external challenges, competitors, or market shifts that could pose risks.

6. **Strategize & Implement:** Based on the SWOT matrix, craft actionable strategies that capitalize on strengths, mitigate weaknesses, harness opportunities, and defend against threats.

 Apple conducts SWOT analyses to identify its strengths, weaknesses, opportunities, and threats in the competitive tech landscape.

Competitive Analysis

How might we

Evaluate competitors' offerings, identifying strengths, weaknesses, and potential opportunities.

What you can do with the method...

Competitive Analysis is a strategic tool that assesses what competitors are doing right and where they might be falling short. By analyzing their features, design, content, and overall user experience, you can identify industry standards, innovative approaches, and potential gaps in the market. This not only benchmarks your product but also offers insights into potential differentiators and areas of opportunity to gain a competitive edge.

Tip

Go beyond surface-level evaluations. Dive deep into user reviews, feedback forums, and social media discussions about competitors. This will provide unfiltered insights into what real users appreciate or dislike, revealing potential areas for differentiation.

 91% of businesses believe that competitive analysis is essential for staying ahead in the market. (Source: Crayon)

Discover and Empathize

Competitive Analysis

How the method is applied

1. **Define Objectives:** Clearly outline what you aim to understand from the analysis, be it feature comparison, user experience, or market positioning.

2. **Identify Competitors:** List direct and indirect competitors. Remember, they might not always be the most obvious choices.

3. **Gather Data:** Use tools, platforms, and manual reviews to collect data on competitor features, designs, user feedback, and more.

4. **Analyze Strengths & Weaknesses:** Evaluate the data, identifying what competitors excel at and where they might have shortcomings.

5. **Spot Opportunities & Threats:** Based on your analysis, pinpoint potential areas where you can innovate, differentiate, or need to be wary of.

6. **Synthesize & Strategize:** Compile findings into a structured report. Use insights to inform your design and business strategies, ensuring you stay ahead in the competitive landscape.

 Tesla regularly analyzes its competitors in the electric vehicle market to identify opportunities for differentiation and innovation.

21

Synthesize and Strategize

In this phase, the gathered insights are synthesized to craft a clear problem statement, define user requirements, and develop a strategic roadmap.

1. Affinity Mapping
2. Task Analysis
3. Jobs To Be Done
4. Value Proposition Design
5. Business Model Canvas
6. Feature Matrix
7. Gap Analysis
8. Kano Model
9. MoSCoW Method
10. Requirement Prioritization

Affinity Mapping

How might we

Organize diverse insights, clustering data into meaningful themes for clearer decision-making.

What you can do with the method...

Affinity Mapping is a collaborative technique used to sort and categorize large amounts of data by drawing out themes or patterns. Typically done with post-it notes on a wall, it's a hands-on activity that encourages team participation. As insights from research or brainstorming sessions are grouped, connections emerge, revealing overarching themes. This visualization aids in understanding complex data sets, fostering clearer discussions, and driving informed design decisions.

Tip

Encourage a judgment-free zone. The initial stages of affinity mapping should focus on clustering without deep analysis. This ensures all perspectives are considered, and unexpected patterns can emerge naturally.

 Affinity mapping can improve team collaboration and idea generation by 50%. (Source: Interaction Design Foundation)

Affinity Mapping

How the method is applied

1. **Gather Insights:** Aggregate raw data, observations, and feedback. This can emerge from user interviews, workshops, or brainstorming sessions.

2. **Prepare Workspace:** Designate a spacious area with a blank wall or board. Equip the space with post-it notes, markers, and any relevant research artifacts.

3. **Distribute & Group Data:** Write individual insights on post-its. As a team, place them on the wall, clustering related insights together without overthinking.

4. **Define Key Themes:** Review each cluster, naming it with a theme or category that encapsulates the grouped insights.

5. **Engage in Dialogue:** Discuss patterns and anomalies within clusters, extracting actionable insights to guide the project.

6. **Document & Implement:** Convert the physical clusters into a digital record. Use derived insights to influence design choices and research directions.

 IBM and SaaS products use affinity mapping to organize and synthesize user research findings and identify common themes.

Task Analysis

How might we

Dissect user tasks, understanding each step's intricacies, to optimize workflows and interfaces.

What you can do with the method...

Task Analysis is the process of breaking down a user's task into its constituent steps to gain a deeper understanding of user workflows. It illuminates the sequence of actions, decisions, and interactions a user undergoes to accomplish a specific goal. By mapping these steps, designers can identify pain points, redundancies, or inefficiencies in a process, making it invaluable for enhancing user experience and optimizing interface designs.

Tip

Always consider the user's context and environment. A task performed on mobile in a rush might differ from the same task on a desktop with ample time. Contextual nuances can significantly influence task flow and potential challenges.

 Task analysis can reduce user errors by 30% by breaking down complex tasks into manageable steps. (Source: Usability.gov)

Task Analysis

How the method is applied

1. **Identify Key Tasks:** Start by listing primary user tasks you want to analyze, often stemming from user goals or objectives.

2. **Observe & Document:** Watch users perform these tasks, noting down each action, decision, and interaction in sequence.

3. **Break Down Steps:** Decompose tasks into detailed, granular steps, ensuring no action, however minor, is overlooked.

4. **Identify Challenges:** Within the detailed task flow, pinpoint areas where users may struggle, hesitate, or encounter inefficiencies.

5. **Optimize Workflow:** Based on identified pain points, brainstorm ways to streamline tasks, reduce steps, or improve interface interactions.

6. **Iterate & Validate:** Implement suggested optimizations and validate with users. Task Analysis is iterative; as user behaviors or tools evolve, revisit and refine your analysis.

 Microsoft conducts task analyses to understand how users complete specific tasks within their software products.

Jobs To Be Done

How might we

Focus on the problems users are trying to solve to create solutions that truly meet their needs.

What you can do with the method...

Jobs To Be Done (JTBD) shifts the focus from user attributes to the "jobs" or tasks that users want to accomplish. By understanding the goals and challenges users face, you can develop features and services that genuinely address those needs. This technique is valuable for product development, feature prioritization, and can even guide marketing strategies.

Tip

While conducting JTBD interviews, probe for the emotional and social dimensions of the job, not just the functional aspects. This will give you a holistic understanding of the user's needs and help you create solutions that resonate on multiple levels.

 Focusing on user's "jobs to be done" framework can lead to a 60% reduction in product development time (Harvard Business Review)

Jobs To Be Done

How the method is applied

1. **Identify Jobs:** Start by listing potential jobs that users are hiring/downloading your product to do.

2. **User Interviews:** Conduct interviews to get insights into the jobs, pains, and gains.

3. **Job Statements:** Formulate clear job statements that define what users are trying to achieve.

4. **Prioritize:** Rank the jobs based on factors like frequency, pain level, and business relevance.

5. **Solution Brainstorm:** Use the prioritized jobs to brainstorm potential solutions or features.

6. **Prototype:** Create prototypes focusing on solving the jobs identified.

7. **Test & Validate:** Conduct usability tests and A/B tests to validate if the solutions meet the job requirements.

8. **Iterate & Improve:** Refine the features based on feedback and keep an eye on how well they're performing the jobs over time.

 Intercom, a customer messaging platform, used JTBD to redesign their onboarding experience. By understanding the key jobs new users were trying to accomplish, such as setting up custom greetings and automating messages, Intercom was able to create a more streamlined and effective onboarding flow that helped users achieve their goals faster.

Value Proposition Design

How might we

Clearly articulate the unique value that our product or service offers, making it irresistible to users.

What you can do with the method...

Value Proposition Design is a strategic tool aimed at ensuring your product or service meets customer needs and solves their problems in a way that is distinct from competitors. It helps in understanding the unique features or experiences that make your offering attractive, allowing you to communicate this value clearly through your design and messaging.

Tip

Don't just focus on features; think about the emotional benefits or peace of mind that your product can offer. Understand the 'gain creators' and 'pain relievers' in your value proposition, and make sure they resonate with your target audience's most significant needs and desires.

 Companies with a clear value proposition experience 2x faster customer growth (Source: CB Insights).

Value Proposition Design

How the method is applied

1. **Customer & Market Research:** Combine customer interviews, surveys, and competitive analysis to understand needs and market gaps.

2. **Craft Value Proposition:** Create a succinct statement that articulates the unique benefits your product offers.

3. **Feature Alignment:** Map out the features and design elements that directly support your value proposition.

4. **Prototype & Messaging:** Develop mockups and messaging that encapsulate the value proposition.

5. **User Validation:** Use targeted testing to confirm the value proposition resonates with your audience.

6. **Iterate & Implement:** Refine the proposition and design based on feedback, and integrate them into your product.

> Airbnb used Value Proposition Design to create a compelling alternative to traditional hotel accommodations. By understanding the jobs, pains, and gains of travelers seeking unique, local experiences, Airbnb designed a platform that connects guests with local hosts, offering a more personalized and authentic travel experience. This value proposition has helped Airbnb differentiate itself from competitors and grow into a global hospitality brand.

Business Model Canvas

How might we

Visually map out and understand a business's value proposition, infrastructure, and customers.

What you can do with the method...

The Business Model Canvas is a strategic management tool that provides a visual framework for developing, describing, and analyzing a business model. Presented in a single view, it captures essential elements like key partners, activities, resources, value propositions, customer relationships, channels, customer segments, cost structure, and revenue streams. It's a vital tool for startups and enterprises alike to iterate and refine their business models.

Tip

Continuously iterate on your canvas. As markets evolve, customer needs shift, or as you learn more about your business, revisit and adjust your canvas to reflect these changes accurately.

 80% of startups that use the Business Model Canvas report a clearer understanding of their business model and strategy. (Source: Strategyzer)

Business Model Canvas

How the method is applied

1. **Start with Value Proposition:** Define the unique value your business offers to customers.

2. **Identify Key Partners & Resources:** List essential partnerships and resources needed for your business operations.

3. **Detail Key Activities:** Describe the main activities required to create and deliver your value proposition.

4. **Delineate Customer Segments:** Identify and segment your target audience based on their needs and behaviors.

5. **Define Channels & Relationships:** Specify how you'll reach your customers and the type of relationship you'll establish.

6. **Determine Cost Structure:** Outline the major costs and expenses associated with running your business.

7. **Predict Revenue Streams:** Identify potential revenue sources and how you'll monetize your value proposition.

 Startup's use the Business Model Canvas to define and iterate on their business strategy in the early stages of the company.

Feature Matrix

How might we

Visually compare features across products, ensuring informed decisions and competitive positioning.

What you can do with the method...

A Feature Matrix is a comparison tool that visually lays out features across different products or versions. It offers a clear snapshot of where a product stands in relation to competitors or its previous versions. By mapping out features in a grid format, teams can quickly identify gaps, overlaps, or unique selling points. This tool is invaluable for product development, marketing strategies, and stakeholder communications, offering a clear, concise view of product capabilities.

Tip

Always keep your target audience in mind. A matrix for internal team discussions might differ from one created for potential customers. Tailor the depth and granularity of features listed based on the audience's expertise and needs.

 Using a feature matrix can help prioritize features and improve product planning by 30%. (Source: Product Management Institute)

Feature Matrix

How the method is applied

1. **Define Objective:** Understand the goal behind the matrix, be it competitor analysis, version comparison, or stakeholder communication.

2. **List Features:** Enumerate all potential features you want to compare, ensuring comprehensive coverage.

3. **Select Products/Versions:** Decide on the products or versions you want to compare against. These could be competitors, older versions, or market leaders.

4. **Create the Grid:** Design a matrix with products/versions as columns and features as rows. Mark presence or absence of each feature for every product.

5. **Analyze & Identify Gaps:** Study the matrix to identify where your product excels, lacks, or matches competitors.

6. **Iterate & Update:** A Feature Matrix is dynamic. As products evolve or new competitors emerge, update the matrix to ensure it remains relevant and accurate.

 Asana uses a feature matrix to prioritize and roadmap new features based on user needs and business objectives.

Gap Analysis

How might we

Identify disparities between current states and desired outcomes, guiding strategic planning.

What you can do with the method...

GAP Analysis is a method used to pinpoint discrepancies between the existing state of a project, product, or process and its desired or potential state. By recognizing these "gaps," teams can develop actionable strategies to bridge them. The analysis aids in understanding shortcomings, areas of improvement, and untapped opportunities. It's a pivotal tool in strategic planning, ensuring resources are channeled effectively to achieve set objectives.

Tip

GAP Analysis is not just about spotting the discrepancies; it's equally crucial to understand the underlying reasons for these gaps. Delving into the 'why' can yield actionable insights and more targeted solutions.

Gap analysis can identify up to 50% of the areas for improvement in business processes and strategies. (Source: Harvard Business Review)

Gap Analysis

How the method is applied

1. **State the Current Situation:** Clearly define and document the present state of the process, product, or performance.

2. **Define the Desired Outcome:** Articulate the goal, target, or ideal state you aim to achieve.

3. **Identify Gaps:** Compare the current situation with the desired outcome to spot discrepancies or shortfalls.

4. **Analyze Root Causes:** Dive deeper into each identified gap to understand its underlying causes. This might involve stakeholder interviews, data analysis, or market research.

5. **Develop Action Plans:** Based on root causes, formulate strategies or steps to bridge the gaps. This could involve process changes, resource allocation, or new initiatives.

6. **Implement & Monitor:** Execute the action plans, continuously monitoring progress. Adjust strategies as needed, ensuring the gap narrows and desired outcomes are achieved.

 Organizations conduct gap analyses to identify opportunities for new product offerings and improvements to existing products.

Kano Model

How might we

Categorize product features based on user satisfaction and their impact on overall experience.

What you can do with the method...

The Kano Model is a framework that helps prioritize product features by categorizing them into 'Basic', 'Performance', and 'Delightful'. It evaluates how certain features influence user satisfaction. 'Basic' features are expected and might cause dissatisfaction if absent. 'Performance' features have a direct correlation with satisfaction. 'Delightful' features, when present, can significantly boost satisfaction but won't cause much dissatisfaction if absent.

Tip

While the Kano Model provides structure, it's essential to revisit categorizations regularly. User expectations evolve, and what's 'Delightful' today might become 'Basic' tomorrow.

 The Kano Model can increase customer satisfaction by 20% by identifying and prioritizing features that delight users. (Source: 280 Group)

Kano Model

How the method is applied

1. **Gather Features List:** Enumerate all potential features or attributes of the product or service.

2. **Design Questionnaire:** For each feature, create two questions - functional (if the feature exists) and dysfunctional (if it doesn't).

3. **Survey Users:** Administer the questionnaire to a representative user group, capturing their feelings about the presence or absence of each feature.

4. **Categorize Responses:** Based on user feedback, categorize each feature as 'Basic', 'Performance', or 'Delightful'.

5. **Prioritize Development:** Allocate resources to 'Basic' features first as they are foundational. Then focus on high-impact 'Performance' features, followed by 'Delightful' ones.

6. **Iterate & Re-evaluate:** Post-launch, gather user feedback and re-evaluate feature categorizations, adjusting development priorities as user needs and market dynamics evolve.

 Enterprises use the Kano Model to prioritize features based on their potential to delight customers.

MoSCoW Method

How might we

Prioritize requirements by categorizing them based on their significance and urgency.

What you can do with the method...

The MoSCoW Method is a prioritization technique used to segregate requirements into four categories: must-have, should-have, could-have, and won't-have. It aids teams in understanding what's vital for a project's success versus what's nice-to-have or can be deferred. By clearly defining the importance of each requirement, it ensures that projects remain focused, stakeholders are aligned, and resources are optimally utilized to deliver the highest value.

Tip

Engage stakeholders regularly in the MoSCoW process to ensure alignment. While 'must'-haves' are critical, resist the urge to overload this category. Over-prioritizing can lead to resource strain and diluted focus. Strive for balance, ensuring that each category is populated with thoughtful consideration to maintain project agility.

 The MoSCoW method can improve project prioritization and delivery by 25%. (Source: Project Management Institute)

MoSCoW Method

How the method is applied

1. **List All Requirements:** Start by documenting every feature, function, or requirement for your project.

2. **Collaborative Session:** Organize a session with stakeholders, project managers, and team members.

3. **Categorize 'Must Haves':** Identify non-negotiables critical for the project's success. Without these, the project would fail.

4. **Determine 'Should Haves':** Features important but not vital. Their absence won't halt the project but would reduce its value.

5. **Outline 'Could Haves':** Desirable features that, if time permits, could be included but can be postponed without significant impact.

6. **Pinpoint 'Won't Haves':** Features agreed upon to be excluded from the current iteration but could be considered for the future.

7. **Review & Refine:** Regularly revisit the categorizations, adjusting based on project evolution, stakeholder feedback, or resource availability.

 The BBC uses the MoSCoW Method to prioritize requirements for its digital products and services.

Requirement Prioritization

How might we

Determine and rank the most crucial requirements, ensuring project alignment and resource optimization.

What you can do with the method...

Requirements Prioritization is pivotal in project management and design. It's the process of assessing, ranking, and determining the sequence of feature or requirement implementation. By understanding the importance, value, and feasibility of each requirement, teams can align their efforts towards what matters most. This tool aids in maximizing returns, managing stakeholders' expectations, and ensuring resources are efficiently utilized on high-impact tasks.

Tip

Involve diverse team members in the prioritization process. Different perspectives, from development to design to business, can provide a holistic view of requirement importance and feasibility.

 Effective requirement prioritization can reduce project scope creep by 30%. (Source: PMI)

Requirement Prioritization

How the method is applied

1. **List All Requirements:** Start by documenting every feature, function, or requirement expected in the project.

2. **Define Criteria:** Determine criteria for prioritization, such as user impact, business value, cost, or feasibility.

3. **Rank Requirements:** Using the criteria, assign scores or ranks to each requirement. This can be done collaboratively.

4. **Categorize & Group:** Segregate requirements into categories like 'Must-Have', 'Should-Have', 'Could-Have', and 'Won't-Have' based on their ranks.

5. **Review with Stakeholders:** Engage stakeholders in discussions around the prioritized list, ensuring alignment with business goals and user needs.

6. **Iterate & Finalize:** Based on feedback and any project changes, re-evaluate and adjust the prioritized list as necessary, ensuring it remains aligned with project objectives.

 Salesforce uses requirement prioritization techniques to ensure its products meet the most critical needs of its customers.

Conceptualize and Innovate

This phase involves unleashing creativity, generating a wide range of innovative ideas, and exploring potential solutions to the defined problem.

1. Brainstorming
2. Concept Mapping
3. Mind Mapping
4. Sketching
5. Storyboarding
6. Scenario Development
7. Six Thinking Hats
8. Design Thinking
9. Lean UX
10. Service Design
11. Participatory Design

Brainstorming

How might we

Generate a plethora of ideas, fostering creativity and team collaboration.

What you can do with the method...

Brainstorming is a group creativity technique designed to generate a wide array of ideas for problem-solving. It's about fostering an open, collaborative environment where all ideas, no matter how outlandish, are welcomed. This free-flowing, dynamic process can lead to innovative solutions, often combining or building upon the diverse thoughts of participants. It's a foundational tool in ideation, used across industries to spark innovation.

Tip

The best brainstorming sessions thrive on diversity and openness. Foster an environment where every idea, no matter how unconventional, is valued. Remember, it's quantity over quality at this stage; refinement comes later. The goal is to unlock creativity and see where it leads.

 Brainstorming can increase idea generation by 50%, fostering creativity and innovation. (Source: Harvard Business Review)

Brainstorming

How the method is applied

1. **Define the Objective:** Clearly articulate the problem or topic, ensuring all participants are aligned.

2. **Assemble a Diverse Group:** A mix of backgrounds and expertise can lead to richer ideas and perspectives.

3. **Set Ground Rules:** Emphasize non-judgment, openness, and the importance of every contribution, no matter how unconventional.

4. **Capture Every Thought:** Utilize whiteboards, sticky notes, or digital tools to record ideas, ensuring all are visible.

5. **Group & Categorize Ideas:** Post-session, cluster ideas into themes, identifying potential patterns or standout solutions.

6. **Determine Next Steps:** Collaboratively decide which ideas to pursue further, setting clear actions and responsibilities.

 IDEO is known for its creative brainstorming sessions, which have led to innovative product ideas and solutions.

Concept Mapping

How might we

Visually organize and represent knowledge about a specific topic or concept.

What you can do with the method...

Concept Mapping is a visual tool that represents the relationships between ideas or concepts. It aids in understanding complex topics by breaking them down into interconnected components. By visually linking related concepts, one can quickly grasp the structure of a subject, see patterns, and identify gaps. This tool is invaluable in education, brainstorming sessions, and when planning or structuring content in various fields.

Tip

Start with a central idea and radiate outward. Allow for flexibility; as you map, you might discover new connections or need to reposition concepts to better reflect their relationships.

 Concept mapping can improve understanding and retention of information by 23%. (Source: Journal of Educational Psychology)

Concept Mapping

How the method is applied

1. **Identify Central Topic:** Begin with a core concept or topic you want to explore.

2. **Brainstorm Sub-concepts:** List out related ideas or subtopics connected to the central topic.

3. **Draw Initial Nodes:** Represent each concept with circles or boxes on a blank canvas.

4. **Connect Nodes:** Using lines, connect related concepts. Label the lines to describe the nature of the relationship.

5. **Layer the Information:** Place foundational or broad concepts at the top or center, with more specific or detailed ideas branching out.

6. **Review & Refine:** Examine the map for clarity and accuracy. Adjust as necessary, ensuring that relationships are clear and logically organized.

7. **Share & Collaborate:** Present the concept map to peers or stakeholders, inviting feedback and additional insights to enrich the map.

 NASA uses concept mapping to break down complex systems and processes into more manageable components.

Mind Mapping

How might we

Visually organize information, fostering clarity and sparking creative insights.

What you can do with the method...

Mind mapping is a visual tool to represent thoughts, ideas, tasks, or other items linked to a central concept. It's instrumental in brainstorming sessions, planning projects, or structuring complex information. The hierarchical and associative nature of mind maps aids in understanding, recall, and generation of new ideas. By visually organizing information, it facilitates clearer thinking and boosts creativity.

Tip

Start with a central idea and let your thoughts flow freely. Use colors, symbols, and images to differentiate and emphasize concepts. The more visual, the better.

 Mind mapping can boost productivity by 25% by helping organize thoughts and ideas more effectively. (Source: Mind Mapping Software Blog)

Mind Mapping

How the method is applied

1. **Choose a Central Idea:** Begin with a primary concept or problem statement in the center of your canvas.

2. **Branch Out Major Themes:** Draw lines from the center, representing main categories or themes related to the central idea.

3. **Expand with Sub-Topics:** For each major theme, branch out further with related sub-topics or specific ideas.

4. **Incorporate Visuals:** Add images, symbols, or colors to enhance recall and stimulate creativity.

5. **Iterate and Refine:** As you progress, rearrange, add, or eliminate branches to better represent the information hierarchy.

6. **Collaborate and Discuss:** Share the mind map with peers or stakeholders. Use it as a discussion tool to gather insights, feedback, or further expand on concepts.

> Disney uses mind mapping to generate and organize ideas for new movies, characters, and theme park attractions.

Sketching

How might we

Quickly visualize and iterate on design concepts for clarity and innovation.

What you can do with the method...

Sketching is a fundamental tool in the design process, allowing for rapid visualization of ideas. Whether it's a product's layout, an app's user interface, or a web page structure, sketching brings abstract concepts to life. It fosters quick iterations, promotes feedback, and acts as a springboard for more refined designs. Its low-fidelity nature ensures that the focus remains on functionality and flow rather than aesthetics.

Tip

Embrace imperfections in sketches. They're meant to be fluid and adaptable. Prioritize capturing the essence of the idea rather than creating polished drawings.

 Sketching can speed up the ideation process by 25%, allowing for quick visualization of concepts. (Source: Design Council)

Sketching

How the method is applied

1. **Gather Supplies:** Ensure you have sketching tools like pencils, markers, and paper or digital tools if preferred.

2. **Define Purpose:** Understand the problem or concept you aim to visualize. Is it a user flow, a layout, or an interface element?

3. **Brainstorm Freely:** Allow yourself to sketch without inhibition. Explore multiple variations and perspectives.

4. **Iterate Rapidly:** Refine sketches based on feedback, new insights, or evolving requirements. Make quick adjustments.

5. **Collaborate & Share:** Use sketches as a communication tool. Share with team members, stakeholders, or users for feedback.

6. **Transition to Higher Fidelity:** Once the sketch meets the desired direction, use it as a foundation for wireframes, mockups, or prototypes, translating the concept into a more refined design.

> Apple is known for its extensive use of sketching in the early stages of product design to quickly visualize and iterate on ideas.

Storyboarding

How might we

Visually narrate user interactions, capturing the flow and emotional journey of an experience.

What you can do with the method...

Storyboarding is a visual technique used to depict the user's journey through a series of illustrated panels, much like a comic strip. It captures the sequence of interactions, emotions, and decision points a user encounters. Designers use storyboards to envision and communicate how a user might interact with a product or service, making abstract concepts tangible and fostering empathetic design solutions.

Tip

Remember, storyboarding isn't about artistic prowess but clarity of communication. Focus on capturing the essence of user interactions and emotions, not perfect illustrations.

 Storyboarding can improve project clarity and communication by 50%, reducing misunderstandings and errors. (Source: Project Management Institute)

Storyboarding

How the method is applied

1. **Define the Scenario:** Identify the user experience or process you want to explore and illustrate.

2. **List Key Moments:** Break down the experience into pivotal moments or interactions the user will encounter.

3. **Sketch the Panels:** Draw out each moment, keeping illustrations simple but clear, showing user actions and emotions.

4. **Incorporate Annotations:** Add brief notes or descriptions below each panel to provide context or highlight specific design considerations.

5. **Present & Gather Feedback:** Share the storyboard with stakeholders or team members to gather insights and identify potential improvements.

6. **Refine & Iterate:** Based on feedback, adjust the storyboard or the design concepts it represents, ensuring the user's journey is clear and intuitive.

 Pixar uses storyboarding to plan and visualize the narrative flow of its animated films.

Conceptualize and Innovate

Scenario Development

How might we

Envision potential user interactions, understanding their context, motivations, and outcomes.

What you can do with the method...

Scenario Development is a narrative tool that crafts hypothetical situations where a user interacts with a product or service. By creating these stories, designers can anticipate user needs, behaviors, and potential challenges. Scenarios paint a vivid picture of the user's context, goals, and actions, guiding design decisions and ensuring that solutions are aligned with user expectations and real-world use cases.

Tip

Craft scenarios that are realistic and representative of your target audience. Incorporate insights from user research to ensure authenticity and relevance in the narratives.

 Scenario development can improve user empathy and understanding by 40%, leading to more user-centered designs. (Source: Interaction Design Foundation)

Scenario Development

How the method is applied

1. **Identify Core User:** Start with a distinct user persona, diving deep into their motivations, needs, and background.

2. **Set the Stage:** Describe the specific environment or situation leading to the user's interaction with the product or service.

3. **Detail User Objectives:** Clearly outline the primary goals or tasks the user aims to achieve within this scenario.

4. **Narrate Key Interactions:** Systematically illustrate how the user engages with the product, pinpointing crucial touchpoints and decisions.

5. **Highlight Challenges & Responses:** Shed light on potential obstacles the user might encounter and how they navigate or overcome them.

6. **Conclude & Reflect:** Summarize the outcome of the user's journey and use this narrative as a foundation for design decisions, ensuring solutions are aligned with real-world user experiences.

 Philips uses scenario development to envision how its products will be used in real-world contexts.

Six Thinking Hats

How might we

Employ varied perspectives for comprehensive problem-solving and idea generation.

What you can do with the method...

Edward de Bono created the "Six Thinking Hats" method, which offers a structured approach to thinking and decision-making. Each 'hat' symbolizes a different style of thinking, enabling teams to view issues from multiple angles. By donning different 'hats', participants can shift their thinking, avoiding cognitive biases and fostering holistic solutions. This technique is invaluable in brainstorming sessions, strategy meetings, and problem-solving scenarios.

Tip

While using the method, it's crucial to create an environment where participants feel free to fully immerse in each hat's mindset. The true power of this technique lies in the genuine exploration of diverse perspectives, which can unveil hidden insights and foster innovative solutions.

 Using the Six Thinking Hats method can improve decision-making effectiveness by 20%. (Source: Edward de Bono Institute)

Six Thinking Hats

How the method is applied

1. **Kickoff with Blue Hat:** Begin by setting the session's objectives and laying out the process. Ensure participants understand the problem or topic in focus.

2. **White Hat Gathering:** Dive into facts and raw data. Collect objective information, steering clear of subjective interpretations.

3. **Red Hat Emotions:** Create a safe space for participants to express feelings and intuitions. Encourage genuine sharing without seeking justification.

4. **Green Hat Creativity:** Foster a brainstorming environment. Challenge participants to think laterally, exploring fresh perspectives and alternatives.

5. **Balanced Analysis:** Using the Black Hat, discuss potential risks and challenges. Switch to the Yellow Hat to identify benefits and positive outcomes.

6. **Wrap Up with Blue Hat:** Conclude by summarizing insights. Outline actionable steps and ensure alignment among participants on the way forward.

 Procter & Gamble uses the Six Thinking Hats technique to facilitate creative problem-solving and decision-making.

Design Thinking

How might we

Incorporate a human-centric approach for solving complex problems in product design and development.

What you can do with the method...

Design Thinking is a problem-solving framework that focuses on human needs, iterative testing, and interdisciplinary collaboration. It fosters creative solutions by encouraging empathy, ideation, and prototyping. It's not just for designers; this approach equips any team to tackle challenges more innovatively. It consists of five stages: Empathize, Define, Ideate, Prototype, and Test, providing a model that allows teams to understand their users deeply.

Tip

Don't rush through the phases. Each stage of Design Thinking has it's own significance. Skipping or rushing can lead to missing out on essential insights. The goal is to understand, explore, and iterate; remember, failing fast and early is better than failing late in the process.

 Design thinking can help reduce product development time by up to 70% (IDEO)

Design Thinking

How the method is applied

1. **Empathize:** Conduct user research to understand your audience's needs and problems. Utilize interviews, observations, and surveys.

2. **Define:** Synthesize research findings into problem statements. These should be human-centric, clear, and actionable.

3. **Ideate:** Brainstorm solutions without limitations. Use techniques like mind-mapping, sketching, and role-playing to encourage diverse thinking.

4. **Prototype:** Create low-fidelity models of your solutions. These can range from paper sketches to digital wireframes.

5. **Test:** Put your prototype in front of real users. Observe, take notes, and ask questions to gather qualitative data.

6. **Iterate:** Use the feedback to refine the solution. The Design Thinking process is iterative; go back to previous steps as needed to fine-tune or pivot.

 PillPack, an online pharmacy, used design thinking to reimagine the prescription medication experience. By empathizing with users' challenges, they developed a solution that simplifies medication management by pre-sorting and packaging pills by dose and delivery time.

Conceptualize and Innovate

Lean UX

How might we

Implement a streamlined, agile methodology that prioritizes user experience in an iterative process.

What you can do with the method...

Lean UX integrates lean startup and agile methodologies with traditional UX practices. It focuses on delivering a usable product as quickly as possible by emphasizing rapid prototyping and iterative design. Lean UX minimizes documentation and encourages cross-functional collaboration. By using this approach, you'll adapt to user feedback more quickly, allowing your design to evolve in alignment with user needs and business goals.

Tip

Lean doesn't mean hasty. It's about being smart with your resources. Use minimal viable prototypes to validate assumptions, and remember that data beats opinions. Constant feedback loops with users and stakeholders ensure you're on the right track.

 Lean UX principles can help iterate on designs quickly, leading to a faster time to market (Usability.gov)

Lean UX

How the method is applied

1. **Identify Assumptions:** Start by gathering your team to list all the assumptions about the project's goals, target users, and features. This serves as your starting point.

2. **Formulate Hypotheses:** Transform the most critical assumptions into hypotheses that you can test. Frame them as actionable statements that focus on user behavior and measurable outcomes.

3. **Design Experiments:** Plan the fastest and most straightforward way to test your hypotheses through MVPs (Minimal Viable Products).

4. **Conduct User Research:** Test your MVPs on real users and collect qualitative and quantitative data.

5. **Analyze & Learn:** Convene with your team to analyze the data collected. Identify patterns and insights that inform whether the hypothesis is validated or invalidated.

6. **Iterate or Pivot:** Use the insights to refine your product or change your direction based on validated learning.

 Dropbox used Lean UX principles to redesign their mobile app. By creating MVP prototypes and conducting rapid user testing, the team was able to validate key design decisions and iterate quickly based on user feedback. This approach resulted in a more user-centered design that significantly improved user engagement and satisfaction.

Service Design

How might we

Create seamless and efficient customer experiences by thoroughly understanding and optimizing every aspect of the service journey.

What you can do with the method...

Service Design involves understanding and designing the complete end-to-end experience from a customer's perspective. By mapping out all touchpoints and interactions, you can identify pain points and opportunities for improvement. Service blueprints and journey maps allow you to visualize the entire service process, ensuring alignment across departments and channels. This holistic approach results in a more cohesive and satisfying customer experience.

Tip

Utilize service blueprints and journey maps to visualize and improve customer experiences across all touchpoints. These practices provide a comprehensive view of the service ecosystem, ensuring every interaction is optimized.

 Focusing on service design principles can increase customer satisfaction by 33% (Source: PwC).

Service Design

How the method is applied

1. **Research and Insights:** Gather data through interviews, surveys, and observational research to understand customer needs and pain points.

2. **Journey Mapping:** Create detailed maps of the customer journey, identifying key interactions and emotional states across all touchpoints.

3. **Service Blueprinting:** Develop service blueprints illustrating relationships between front-stage (customer-facing) and back-stage (behind-the-scenes) activities.

4. **Touchpoint Analysis:** Examine each touchpoint for consistency and effectiveness, ensuring alignment with the overall service vision.

5. **Co-Creation Workshops:** Engage stakeholders, including employees and customers, in workshops to collaboratively ideate and prototype service improvements.

6. **Prototyping and Testing:** Develop and test low-fidelity prototypes with real users to gather feedback and refine service concepts.

 Virgin Atlantic employed service design to reimagine their passenger experience, resulting in increased customer satisfaction and loyalty.

Conceptualize and Innovate

Participatory Design

How might we

Create solutions that truly resonate with users by involving them directly in the design process, ensuring their voices and perspectives are integral to the outcome.

What you can do with the method...

Participatory Design involves users and other stakeholders as active participants in the design process. This collaborative method ensures that the resulting product or service aligns closely with user needs and expectations. By involving users in brainstorming, prototyping, and feedback sessions, you can uncover valuable insights and foster a sense of ownership among participants, leading to more innovative and effective solutions.

Tip

Engage stakeholders, including end-users, in the design process to ensure the final product meets their needs and expectations. This collaborative approach fosters innovation and user satisfaction.

 Projects with user involvement can lead to a 20% increase in project success rates (Source: IDEO).

Participatory Design

How the method is applied

1. **Stakeholder Identification:** Identify and recruit a diverse group of stakeholders, including end-users, to participate in the design process.

2. **Workshop Facilitation:** Conduct workshops where stakeholders can share their experiences, ideas, and feedback in a collaborative environment.

3. **Co-Design Sessions:** Engage stakeholders in hands-on design activities, such as sketching, prototyping, and role-playing, to explore different solutions.

4. **Iterative Feedback:** Continuously gather feedback from participants throughout the design process to refine and improve ideas and prototypes.

5. **Prototyping and Testing:** Develop prototypes based on collaborative input and test them with stakeholders to validate concepts and identify areas for improvement.

6. **Implementation and Follow-Up:** Implement the final design with ongoing input from stakeholders and conduct follow-up sessions to gather feedback and assess the impact of the solution.

 The City of Helsinki used participatory design to involve citizens in the redesign of their public services, resulting in more user-centric and accessible solutions.

Envision and Embody

This phase involves unleashing creativity, generating a wide range of innovative ideas, and exploring potential solutions to the defined problem.

1. Rapid Prototyping
2. Paper Prototyping
3. Low-fidelity Prototyping
4. Interactive Wireframes
5. High-fidelity Prototyping
6. Clickable Prototypes
7. Visual Language & Brand Study
8. Animation Timing
9. Color Theory
10. Design Tokens
11. Grid Systems
12. Iconography
13. Micro-interactions
14. Mood Boards
15. Style Guide Development
16. Typography Studies
17. Visual Hierarchy
18. Design System

Rapid Prototyping

How might we

Quickly visualize and test design concepts, iterating based on real-world feedback.

What you can do with the method...

Rapid Prototyping is a design process used to swiftly create a model of a product or system, facilitating user testing and iterative improvement. It allows designers to visualize complex ideas, test their viability, and refine them in real-time. By producing tangible or interactive prototypes, stakeholders can better understand a concept, and potential issues can be identified and addressed early, reducing development costs and time.

Tip

Avoid striving for perfection in initial prototypes. Embrace a 'fail fast, iterate faster' mindset. It's about learning and refining, not producing a final product in the first go.

 Rapid prototyping can reduce development time by 30% by allowing for quick iterations and feedback. (Source: Lean Enterprise Institute)

Rapid Prototyping

How the method is applied

1. **Define Purpose & Scope:** Understand what you aim to achieve with the prototype—be it functionality, design, or overall user experience.

2. **Choose the Right Fidelity:** Decide on the prototype's detail level—low-fidelity sketches or high-fidelity interactive models.

3. **Create the Prototype:** Utilize tools, materials, or software best suited for your chosen fidelity and the concept's complexity.

4. **Conduct User Testing:** Introduce the prototype to a representative user group, collecting feedback on usability and functionality.

5. **Analyze Feedback:** Review the insights gathered, noting areas of success and those needing refinement.

6. **Iterate & Refine:** Based on feedback, make necessary adjustments to the design, and if needed, repeat the testing phase.

 Dyson uses rapid prototyping to quickly test and iterate on new product ideas and designs.

Paper Prototyping

How might we

Quickly visualize and test interactive design ideas without digital constraints.

What you can do with the method...

Paper prototyping is a hands-on, low-tech technique used to visualize and test design concepts. By sketching interfaces, interactions, or even entire products on paper, designers can quickly iterate on ideas without the limitations or time-consuming aspects of digital tools. It's an effective method to gather early user feedback, ensuring that design decisions are user-centric from the very beginning of the design process.

Tip

Incorporate tangible elements like sticky notes or movable paper pieces to simulate interactivity. This not only enhances user engagement during testing but also allows for on-the-spot iterations. Remember, the goal is to emulate real-world interactions as closely as possible, even within the simplicity of paper.

 Paper prototyping can identify 50% of usability issues early in the design process, saving time and resources. (Source: Usability.gov)

Paper Prototyping

How the method is applied

1. **Sketch Your Ideas:** Begin by drawing interface elements, screens, or concepts on paper. Use pencils for flexibility and markers for emphasis.

2. **Define Interactions:** Use separate pieces or overlays to represent interactive elements like buttons, sliders, or pop-ups.

3. **Prepare for Testing:** Identify key tasks or interactions you'd like users to perform with the prototype.

4. **Conduct User Tests:** Engage users, asking them to interact with the paper prototype. Observe their actions, and manually simulate interactions.

5. **Gather Feedback:** Ask users about their experience, any challenges faced, and areas of improvement. Use their feedback for iterations.

6. **Iterate and Refine:** Based on feedback and observations, make adjustments to your design. Repeat the testing process as necessary to validate changes and ensure optimal usability.

 Square has used paper prototyping to test and refine the user experience of its mobile payment app.

Envision and Embody

Low-fidelity Prototyping

How might we

Quickly visualize design concepts without detailed aesthetics or interactions.

What you can do with the method...

Low-fidelity prototypes are basic representations of a design, focusing on function rather than form. They help in mapping out the structure, layout, and user flow of a product, devoid of intricate details, colors, or graphics. This approach is crucial in the early stages of design, allowing swift iterations and facilitating stakeholder feedback without the distractions of a polished design.

Tip

Use low-fidelity prototypes to encourage open feedback. Their simplicity often makes stakeholders and users more willing to suggest changes, knowing that no intricate design work will be discarded.

 Low-fidelity prototyping can speed up the design process by 30% by focusing on core functionality and user flow. (Source: Nielsen Norman Group)

Low-fidelity Prototyping

How the method is applied

1. **Sketch Basic Layouts:** Use paper or digital tools to draft the fundamental structure of each screen.

2. **Define User Journeys:** Mark the basic flow and transitions between different sections or pages.

3. **Keep It Simple:** Avoid detailed visuals. Stick to basic shapes, placeholders, and annotations.

4. **Engage Stakeholders Early:** Present your low-fidelity prototype to stakeholders for initial feedback on structure and flow.

5. **Iterate Swiftly:** The simplicity of these prototypes allows for quick changes based on feedback.

6. **Transition to High-Fidelity:** Once you've refined the structure and flow, begin adding details, eventually transitioning to a high-fidelity prototype.

 Twitter uses low-fidelity prototyping to quickly test and validate new ideas and concepts.

Interactive Wireframes

How might we

Create a clickable model of a design, bridging the gap between static visuals and prototypes.

What you can do with the method...

Interactive wireframes are dynamic blueprints of a digital product, allowing stakeholders and users to experience the flow and interactions of a design without the polished aesthetics. They serve as an intermediary step, making it easier to test, validate, and iterate on functionality and user experience early in the design process. By simulating interactivity, they provide a clearer understanding of the end product.

Tip

Focus on clarity and functionality over aesthetics. Use consistent symbols and annotations, ensuring stakeholders understand every element's purpose.

 Interactive wireframes can reduce design iteration time by 25% by allowing for early user interaction and feedback. (Source: Adobe)

Envision and Embody

Interactive Wireframes

How the method is applied

1. **Start with Static Wireframes:** Draft the basic layout and elements of each screen or page.

2. **Define Interactions:** Specify clickable areas, transitions, and the resulting actions for each interaction.

3. **Use a Tool:** Utilize wireframing tools like Figma, Adobe XD, or InVision to create your interactive wireframes.

4. **Test Flows:** Walk through user journeys to ensure the logical sequence of interactions and smooth transitions.

5. **Gather Feedback:** Share with stakeholders, team members, and potential users. Encourage them to interact with the wireframe and provide insights.

6. **Iterate Based on Feedback:** Refine the wireframe based on the input received, ensuring a seamless and intuitive user experience.

 Airbnb uses interactive wireframes to test and iterate on user flows and interactions.

High-fidelity Prototyping

How might we

Present a detailed, interactive representation of the final product for testing and review.

What you can do with the method...

High-fidelity prototypes offer a detailed and interactive preview of the final product, capturing both design aesthetics and functionality. They reflect actual design choices, from color schemes to typography, and simulate user interactions. These prototypes are invaluable for usability testing, stakeholder reviews, and developer handoffs, ensuring that the end product aligns with the envisioned design.

Tip

High-fidelity doesn't mean final. Stay open to feedback, ensuring that while the design is polished, it remains flexible for necessary iterations based on user testing.

> High-fidelity prototyping can improve stakeholder buy-in by 40% by providing a realistic representation of the final product. (Source: UXPin)

High-fidelity Prototyping

How the method is applied

1. **Incorporate Detailed Designs:** Use tools like Figma or Sketch to craft intricate designs, ensuring they mirror the final aesthetic choices.

2. **Embed Interactions:** Design dynamic elements, such as buttons or dropdowns, to be interactive, simulating the final user experience.

3. **Test User Flows:** Ensure that the navigation and interactions are intuitive and closely resemble the intended final product flow.

4. **Gather Feedback:** Engage stakeholders and users in usability testing sessions, refining the design based on their insights.

5. **Iterate and Refine:** Use feedback to make necessary changes, ensuring the prototype is both user-friendly and aligns with business goals.

6. **Prepare for Development:** Once finalized, use the high-fidelity prototype as a reference for developers, ensuring they understand the design's look and feel.

 Apple creates high-fidelity prototypes to test and refine the look, feel, and functionality of its products before launch.

Clickable Prototypes

How might we

Simulate the actual product experience with interactive elements in a detailed mockup.

What you can do with the method...

Clickable prototypes provide a high-fidelity representation of the final product, allowing users to navigate and interact as they would with the real thing. Unlike static mockups, these prototypes offer a dynamic experience, showcasing transitions, animations, and functionalities. They're essential for usability testing, stakeholder demonstrations, and refining user journeys before diving into development.

Tip

Ensure your prototype feels 'real'. Any deviation from intended design or functionality can skew feedback. Regularly update it based on user tests to refine the experience.

 Clickable prototypes can reduce development time by 20% by allowing for early user testing and feedback. (Source: InVision)

Clickable Prototypes

How the method is applied

1. **Draft High-Fidelity Designs:** Begin with detailed layouts, ensuring they closely resemble the final look.

2. **Identify Interactive Elements:** Mark buttons, links, sliders, and other elements that require interactivity.

3. **Use Prototyping Tools:** Platforms like Figma, Axure, or Sketch offer functionalities to create interactive elements.

4. **Link Screens:** Define the navigation flow by linking different screens or states, ensuring logical transitions.

5. **Test Interactivity:** Navigate through the prototype, validating that interactions align with the intended design and functionality.

6. **Gather User Feedback:** Conduct usability tests, allowing potential users to interact with the prototype. Collect their insights, observations, and feedback to refine further.

 InVision uses clickable prototypes to test and gather feedback on user flows and interactions.

Envision and Embody

Visual Language & Brand Study

How might we

Ensure all visual elements across your product or service consistently reflect your brand identity, creating a strong and recognizable presence.

What you can do with the method...

Visual Language & Brand Study involve creating a consistent set of visual elements that represent your brand. This includes colors, typography, imagery, icons, and layouts. A cohesive visual language enhances brand recognition and ensures a unified user experience. By systematically studying and applying these elements, you can create a visually compelling and memorable brand identity.

Tip

Develop a cohesive visual language that aligns with your brand identity. Consistency in visual elements enhances brand recognition and user trust.

 Consistent visual language can increase brand recognition by 80%. (Source: Lucidpress)

Visual Language & Brand Study

How the method is applied

1. **Brand Identity Analysis:** Study your brand's mission, values, and target audience to understand the core attributes that should be reflected in the visual language.

2. **Style Guide Development:** Create a comprehensive style guide that outlines the rules for using colors, typography, imagery, icons, and other visual elements consistently across all touchpoints.

3. **Mood Boards and Inspiration:** Develop mood boards to capture the desired look and feel of your brand. Use these as inspiration to guide the design of new visual elements.

4. **Prototype and Test:** Design prototypes incorporating the new visual language and test them with users to ensure they effectively communicate the brand and resonate with the audience.

5. **Implementation and Training:** Roll out the new visual language across all platforms and train your team on how to apply the style guide consistently to maintain brand integrity.

 Nike conducts visual language and brand studies to ensure consistency and recognizability across all its products and marketing materials.

Animation Timing

How might we

Craft fluid, intuitive animations that enhance user experiences.

What you can do with the method...

Animation Timing is pivotal in defining the duration and progression of animations in UI/UX design. Properly timed animations guide user attention, clarify relations between elements, and produce delightful interactions. They can make the difference between a jarring and a seamless user experience, enhancing feedback, transitions, and the overall flow of an application.

Tip

Always consider the platform and user context. Faster animations are preferred on mobile, while web can afford slightly longer durations. Ensure that animations don't hinder usability.

 Appropriate animation timing can improve user satisfaction by 25% by creating smooth and intuitive interactions. (Source: Smashing Magazine)

Animation Timing

How the method is applied

1. **Define Purpose:** Understand the role of the animation. Is it for feedback, guiding attention, or purely aesthetic?

2. **Choose Easing:** Decide on the animation's speed curve. Linear, ease-in, ease-out, or custom bezier curves can dramatically affect perception.

3. **Set Duration:** Based on the complexity and type of animation, define how long it should last. Typically, subtle animations range from 200 ms to 500 ms.

4. **Prototype & Test:** Use design tools to prototype animations, ensuring you can tweak timing easily.

5. **Gather Feedback:** Test your animations with real users. Sometimes what feels right to a designer may feel too fast or slow for users.

6. **Iterate & Refine:** Based on feedback, adjust the timing. Consistently test to find the perfect balance that enhances the experience without causing distraction.

 Google uses animation timing to create smooth and engaging transitions in its Material Design system.

Envision and Embody

Color Theory

How might we

Master the art and science of using colors effectively in design.

What you can do with the method...

Color Theory is a fundamental pillar in design, guiding how colors interact, contrast, and complement each other. It dictates the creation of harmonious color schemes, evokes emotional responses, and emphasizes visual hierarchy. By understanding the relationships between hues, tints, tones, and shades, designers can make informed decisions, ensuring their designs are not only aesthetically pleasing but also convey the desired message and mood.

Tip

Colors can evoke emotions and influence user behavior. Always consider cultural context and audience demographics, as color perceptions can vary widely across different groups.

 Effective use of color can increase brand recognition by 80%. (Source: University of Loyola, Maryland)

Color Theory

How the method is applied

1. **Understand Basics:** Learn primary, secondary, and tertiary colors and how they relate on the color wheel.

2. **Explore Relationships:** Dive into color harmonies like complementary, analogous, and triadic schemes.

3. **Consider Context:** Recognize the cultural, demographic, and psychological implications of color choices.

4. **Apply to Design:** Utilize color to highlight importance, create depth, and evoke specific emotions or reactions.

5. **Test & Iterate:** Always test color choices with real users, ensuring accessibility and desired emotional impact.

6. **Stay Updated:** Color trends evolve. Continuously update your knowledge, ensuring your designs remain fresh and relevant.

 Coca-Cola uses color theory to create a consistent and recognizable brand identity across all its products and marketing materials.

Envision and Embody

Design Tokens

How might we

Standardize design values for consistent UI implementation.

What you can do with the method...

Design Tokens are atomic design values (like colors, spacing, and typography) abstracted into named entities, ensuring design consistency across platforms and devices. They act as a bridge between designers and developers, enabling a shared language. Tokens streamline design-to-development handoffs, and when changes are made, they propagate throughout the product, ensuring uniformity.

Tip

Always collaborate closely with developers when defining tokens. This ensures they're feasible for implementation and fit within technical constraints.

 Implementing design tokens can reduce design inconsistencies by 50%, ensuring a cohesive visual language. (Source: Design Systems Handbook)

Design Tokens

How the method is applied

1. **Identify Atomic Values:** Begin by breaking down your design system into its smallest units: colors, font sizes, spacings, etc.

2. **Name the Tokens:** Assign meaningful names that describe their function rather than their value, like "primaryColor" instead of "blue".

3. **Centralize Token Storage:** Store tokens in a centralized system, ensuring easy access and updates for both designers and developers.

4. **Integrate with Tools:** Use tools like Style Dictionary to convert tokens into platform-specific formats.

5. **Regularly Update:** As the product evolves, revisit and update tokens to reflect design changes.

6. **Collaboration is Key:** Maintain open communication channels between designers and developers to ensure tokens remain relevant and useful.

 Salesforce uses design tokens to ensure consistency and maintainability across its design system.

Grid Systems

How might we

Create structured, balanced layouts that enhance visual hierarchy and readability.

What you can do with the method...

Grid Systems are foundational frameworks in design, providing a structured layout for content placement, ensuring alignment, consistency, and balance. By dividing space into columns and rows, grids enable designers to organize elements in a harmonious manner, enhancing visual flow and improving user comprehension. Whether for web or print, a well-implemented grid aids in achieving a clean, organized, and aesthetically pleasing result.

Tip

Maintain consistent gutter widths and column sizes. This uniformity reinforces visual coherence and ensures your content remains organized and easily digestible.

 Using grid systems can improve design alignment and consistency by 30%. (Source: Smashing Magazine)

Grid Systems

How the method is applied

1. **Determine Content Structure:** Assess the content hierarchy and the elements that need emphasis.

2. **Choose Grid Type:** Decide between column grids, modular grids, or hierarchical grids based on design needs.

3. **Define Column & Gutter Widths:** Establish consistent measurements to ensure balanced spacing and alignment.

4. **Place Key Elements:** Position primary design elements, like headers and main content, adhering to the grid's structure.

5. **Add Secondary Elements:** Populate remaining spaces with secondary or tertiary content, ensuring everything aligns with the grid.

6. **Review & Adjust:** Examine the overall layout, ensuring the grid enhances readability and visual appeal. Make adjustments as necessary for optimal results.

> The New York Times uses a grid system to create a consistent and readable layout for its digital content.

Iconography

How might we

Understand the essence and effective application of visual symbols.

What you can do with the method...

Iconography involves crafting and utilizing symbols that represent concepts, actions, or themes. In the realm of design, it's a potent tool, translating abstract ideas into recognizable graphics. These visual elements, when employed effectively, can enhance user comprehension, minimize language barriers, and streamline interface interactions. It's not just about aesthetics; it's about creating an intuitive user journey.

Tip

Always prioritize clarity over intricacy. An effective icon should convey its meaning instantly, even without textual support. Regularly test your icons with diverse users to ensure universal comprehension.

 Consistent iconography can improve user comprehension by 20%. (Source: Nielsen Norman Group)

Iconography

How the method is applied

1. **Research and Inspiration:** Begin by understanding the context and studying successful icon sets.

2. **Sketch Ideas:** Before digitizing, draft various symbols to represent the concept.

3. **Simplicity is Key:** Design icons with clear and uncomplicated visuals. Avoid unnecessary details.

4. **Maintain Consistency:** Ensure a coherent style, stroke weight, and size across the icon set.

5. **Test with Users:** Validate that your icons resonate with the target audience and are easily understood.

6. **Iterate Based on Feedback:** Refine icons based on real-world usage and feedback, ensuring they remain effective and clear.

> Microsoft uses iconography to create a consistent and intuitive visual language across its products and services.

Micro-interactions

How might we

Enhance user experience through small, engaging design details.

What you can do with the method...

Micro-interactions are subtle design elements that fulfill singular tasks, guiding users and giving feedback. These can be a button animation upon clicking, a vibration when a task completes, or a visual cue indicating a change. They enrich user experience by making digital interfaces feel more human, intuitive, and engaging, bridging the gap between user actions and system responses.

Tip

Micro-interactions shouldn't overshadow the main task. They must be intuitive, seamless, and serve a clear purpose to enhance the user's journey without distracting.

 Well-designed micro-interactions can increase user engagement by 30%. (Source: UX Design Institute)

Micro-interactions

How the method is applied

1. **Identify the Need:** Pinpoint areas where feedback or guidance is necessary for the user.

2. **Design Simplicity:** Ensure the interaction is straightforward and doesn't complicate the user's task.

3. **Feedback is Key:** Use micro-interactions as immediate feedback for user actions, reassuring them.

4. **Consistency Matters:** Maintain a consistent style for micro-interactions throughout the interface.

5. **Test and Refine:** Continuously test these interactions to ensure they enhance, not hinder, the user experience.

6. **Iterate:** Based on feedback, continuously improve and refine to keep the interactions fresh and effective.

> Slack uses micro-interactions to provide feedback and enhance the user experience of its platform.

Mood Boards

How might we

Visually convey the intended atmosphere and style of a project.

What you can do with the method...

Mood Boards are visual collages that capture the essence, mood, and inspiration for a project. Comprising images, colors, typography, and other design elements, they serve as a reference point, ensuring that stakeholders share a unified vision. They're invaluable during the initial design phase, helping to communicate abstract ideas, set design directions, and foster a clear understanding of the project's aesthetic and emotional goals.

Tip

Always consider your audience when curating a mood board. It should resonate with both the client's vision and the target users' expectations, striking a balance between aspiration and relatability.

 Mood boards can improve design alignment and inspiration by 25%. (Source: Canva)

Mood Boards

How the method is applied

1. **Define the Purpose:** Understand the project's goals and what you aim to communicate through the mood board.

2. **Gather Inspiration:** Source images, color palettes, typography, textures, and other elements that align with the project's tone.

3. **Curate & Organize:** Select the most relevant materials, ensuring they cohesively represent the desired mood and style.

4. **Arrange Elements:** Place items thoughtfully, considering visual flow, balance, and emphasis.

5. **Review with Stakeholders:** Present the mood board to team members and clients, gathering feedback to ensure alignment with the project's vision.

6. **Iterate & Finalize:** Refine based on feedback, ensuring the board accurately captures and communicates the intended mood and direction.

 Nike creates mood boards to establish the visual direction and aesthetic for its product campaigns and designs.

Style Guide Development

How might we

Establish a unified design language, ensuring consistency across products.

What you can do with the method...

Style Guide Development is a foundational step in creating a cohesive design language for brands or products. It serves as a reference that details the visual and sometimes functional elements of a design, from typography and color palettes to UI components and spacing. This ensures design consistency, facilitates collaboration, and streamlines the design-to-development process.

Tip

Regularly update your style guide to keep it relevant. Engaging multidisciplinary teams in its creation offers diverse perspectives, ensuring a comprehensive and adaptable guide. It's not just a document but an evolving tool that adapts to changing design and brand needs.

 Developing a style guide can reduce design inconsistencies by 40%. (Source: InVision)

Style Guide Development

How the method is applied

1. **Audit Designs:** Review current assets to pinpoint recurring design elements. This forms the basis of your guide.

2. **Define Core Elements:** Detail color palettes, typography scales, and UI components. Consistency in these areas is crucial.

3. **Set Usage Guidelines:** Specify when and how to use elements. It's essential for uniformity across different design phases.

4. **Prioritize Accessibility:** Ensure designs cater to all, with guidelines on color contrast, font choices, and interactive components.

5. **Collaborate:** Engage team members in diverse roles. Their feedback ensures the guide is comprehensive and adaptable.

6. **Maintain the Guide:** As brand needs evolve, update the guide. It's a living document that should reflect the latest design philosophy.

 Airbnb has developed a comprehensive style guide to ensure consistency and cohesion across its brand and products.

Envision and Embody

Typography Studies

How might we

Delve deep into the art and technique of arranging type effectively.

What you can do with the method...

Typography Studies encompass the design, arrangement, and application of type. It's more than just choosing fonts; it's about ensuring readability, creating mood, and setting the personality of the content. Proper typography can elevate a design, guide readers, emphasize important elements, and provide a cohesive visual experience. It's a crucial tool for communicating messages with clarity and aesthetic appeal.

Tip

Good typography is invisible, but bad typography is glaringly obvious. Prioritize readability and consistency, and remember that typeface choices can evoke emotions and set tone.

 Effective typography can improve readability and user comprehension by 20%. (Source: Smashing Magazine)

Typography Studies

How the method is applied

1. **Learn Fundamentals:** Understand type anatomy, including terms like baseline, x-height, and leading.

2. **Choose Typefaces:** Select fonts that align with the design's purpose and audience, considering serifs, sans-serifs, and decorative options.

3. **Set Hierarchy:** Use varying weights, sizes, and styles to guide readers and emphasize key information.

4. **Ensure Readability:** Adjust line spacing, letter spacing, and column width for optimal legibility.

5. **Consider Context:** Different mediums, like print and digital, may require different typographic considerations.

6. **Test & Refine:** Regularly assess typography choices in various contexts, ensuring legibility and desired impact across all platforms

 Medium conducts typography studies to optimize readability and create a distinct typographic style for its platform.

Visual Hierarchy

How might we

Master the art of guiding viewers' attention through design elements.

What you can do with the method...

Visual hierarchy is the arrangement and presentation of design elements in order of their importance. It directs the viewer's eye, ensuring that they absorb information in the intended sequence. By playing with size, color, contrast, and positioning, designers can emphasize key elements, making interfaces more intuitive. This hierarchy enhances user experience by creating a flow that feels natural and logical.

Tip

The most critical information should stand out. Use size, contrast, and space effectively to guide the viewer's eye in a predetermined sequence, ensuring clarity and comprehension.

 Proper visual hierarchy can improve user navigation and task completion by 30%. (Source: Nielsen Norman Group)

Visual Hierarchy

How the method is applied

1. **Define the Message:** Understand the core message and prioritize content.

2. **Play with Size:** Larger elements naturally draw more attention than smaller ones.

3. **Use Contrast:** Differences in color, shape, or texture can highlight or downplay elements.

4. **Manipulate Spacing:** Space can separate or group elements, affecting how they're perceived.

5. **Experiment with Position:** Elements placed centrally or at the top typically get more attention.

6. **Consistent Styling:** Ensure elements of the same importance level have similar styling to avoid confusion.

7. **Feedback and Iteration:** After designing, gather feedback to see if viewers' attention flows as intended and iterate accordingly.

 Apple uses visual hierarchy to guide users' attention and prioritize key information in its product designs.

Design System

How might we

Create a consistent, cohesive, and scalable visual language and interaction patterns across all our products and touch points?

What you can do with the method...

A Design System is a collection of reusable components, guidelines, and standards that define the look, feel, and behavior of a product or family of products. It helps to create a consistent and cohesive user experience across all touch points and products.

Tip

Use a modular and flexible design system that can adapt to changing user needs and business requirements over time.

 Google's Material Design is a comprehensive design system that provides a set of guidelines, components, and tools that help designers and developers create consistent and cohesive user experiences across all of Google's products and platforms.

Design System

How the method is applied

1. **Audit and Inventory:** Audit existing design elements and create an inventory of reusable components and patterns.

2. **Design Principles:** Define the guiding principles and values that will inform the design system.

3. **Component Library:** Create a library of reusable components, such as buttons, forms, and navigation elements.

4. **Style Guide:** Develop a style guide that defines the visual language, including colors, typography, and iconography.

5. **Pattern Library:** Create a library of common user interface patterns, such as search, filtering, and data visualization.

6. **Documentation:** Document the design system, including guidelines for use, best practices, and examples.

7. **Governance:** Establish governance processes to manage the evolution and maintenance of the design system over time.

8. **Follow Atomic Design Methodology**: Atoms, molecules, organisms, templates, and pages

Evaluate and Refine

This phase involves rigorously testing the prototypes with users, gathering valuable feedback, and iteratively refining the designs based on data-driven insights.

1. Usability Testing
2. A/B Testing
3. Guerrilla Testing
4. Wizard of Oz Testing
5. Responsive Design Testing
6. Heuristic Evaluation
7. Cognitive Walkthrough
8. Usability Checklist
9. In-person Observations
10. Remote Usability Tests
11. Eye Tracking
12. Heatmaps
13. Analytics Monitoring
14. Customer Satisfaction Score
15. Net Promoter Score
16. System Usability Scale
17. Time-on-task Measurement
18. Error Rate Measurement

Usability Testing

How might we

Observe how real users interact with a product, pinpointing usability strengths and weaknesses.

What you can do with the method...

Usability Testing offers a live window into user behavior with your product. By setting specific tasks, you watch users navigate, revealing where they face friction or delight. Direct feedback from these sessions provides a roadmap for design improvements. It's not just about finding issues but understanding their root cause, allowing designers to make informed decisions on iterations.

Tip

Test early and frequently; insights from even initial designs can be invaluable. Ensure a diverse participant group for well-rounded feedback. During sessions, be an observer; refrain from leading users, capture genuine interactions.

> Usability testing can identify 85% of usability issues, making it a critical step in the design process. (Source: Nielsen Norman Group)

Usability Testing

How the method is applied

1. **Define Objectives:** Highlight primary interactions and scenarios for assessment.

2. **Recruit Participants:** Select users representing different user personas, ensuring varied feedback.

3. **Environment Setup:** Decide on remote or in-lab sessions. Ensure users are comfortable, with tools ready for capturing insights.

4. **Run the Test:** Assign tasks without guidance on execution. Observe user paths, noting difficulties or ease points.

5. **Post-Test Discussion:** Engage participants about their journey, extracting deeper insights on observed behaviors.

6. **Analysis:** Collate data, identifying common friction points and user challenges. Translate these observations into actionable design improvements.

 Airbnb conducts usability testing to identify pain points and improve the user experience of its website and mobile app.

A/B Testing

How might we

Empirically test variations of a design and measure which performs better for a given objective.

What you can do with the method...

A/B Testing, or split testing, is a potent tool for comparing two design variations to see which resonates more with users. By randomly presenting Version A or B to users, you can gauge which one achieves better outcomes for metrics like click-through rates or conversions. It takes the guesswork out of design decisions, grounding them in real user data, ensuring that iterations genuinely enhance user experience and outcomes.

Tip

Ensure that you're only testing one variable at a time for clear results. For instance, if you're testing a call-to-action button's color, don't change its text simultaneously. Consistency in testing conditions is crucial, and remember to gather a statistically significant sample size before drawing conclusions.

 A/B testing can improve conversion rates by up to 49%, making it a powerful tool for optimizing user experiences. (Source: Invesp)

A/B Testing

How the method is applied

1. **Set Clear Goals:** Decide the specific metric you want to enhance, whether it's user engagement, sign-ups, or another conversion.

2. **Design Two Versions:** Create two distinct versions of the design element, ensuring just one variation between them to isolate its impact.

3. **Route User Traffic:** Use testing platforms to evenly split incoming users, sending half to Version A and half to Version B.

4. **Monitor & Record:** Observe user behaviors with each version, tracking crucial metrics such as click rates, dwell time, or completed actions.

5. **Analyze Data:** After a sufficient sample size and time, review data to determine which version achieved better outcomes for the target metric.

6. **Adopt & Refine:** Implement the superior design. Remember, A/B Testing is cyclical; even after one test concludes, there's always room for further optimization and testing.

 Amazon conducts extensive A/B testing on its website to optimize product placement, pricing, and user experience.

Guerrilla Testing

How might we

Quickly validate design decisions during the wireframing and prototyping stages to ensure the final design is user-centric and meets user needs effectively.

What you can do with the method...

Guerrilla testing is especially crucial during wireframing and prototyping because it provides rapid, real-world input that can steer the design direction. By presenting wireframes and prototypes to real users in informal settings, designers can identify usability issues and gather insights that can refine the product's design.

Tip

Incorporate guerrilla testing into the wireframing and prototyping phases to validate design concepts early and frequently. This lean approach provides immediate user feedback, which is invaluable in shaping the evolution of your wireframes and prototypes. Flexibility is key; be ready to adapt your prototypes based on feedback received.

 Guerrilla testing can uncover 70% of usability issues with minimal cost and time investment. (Source: Nielsen Norman Group)

Guerrilla Testing

How the method is applied

1. **Prepare Wireframes/Prototypes:** Have your wireframes or prototypes ready for quick testing. These can be low-fidelity to encourage focus on the overall concept and usability rather than details.

2. **Engage Users:** Find participants in settings where your potential users naturally occur and ask them to complete tasks using your wireframes or prototypes.

3. **Collect Feedback:** Observe the interactions and listen to the feedback. Take note of where users encounter issues or experience confusion.

4. **Iterate Designs:** Use the insights to make immediate, informed updates to your wireframes and prototypes.

5. **Validate Changes:** Re-test with new users to see if changes have improved the user experience.

6. **Document Findings:** Keep records of feedback and iterations. This helps track the evolution of your designs and supports future decision-making.

 Dropbox has used guerrilla testing to gather quick user feedback on new features and designs.

Wizard of Oz Testing

How might we

Evaluate a system's design by simulating its functionality without actual system operations.

What you can do with the method...

Wizard of Oz Testing allows designers to test systems before they're fully functional. Users believe they're interacting with a working system, but behind the scenes, human "wizards" manually operate the system's responses. This method is vital for gauging user reactions to new features or systems without investing in full development, making it cost-effective and time-efficient for early-stage testing.

Tip

Ensure the 'wizard' remains consistent in responses, mimicking what a fully automated system would offer. Any variation could skew results, so preparation is key.

 Wizard of Oz testing can provide 40% more insights into user behavior by simulating real interactions. (Source: Interaction Design Foundation)

Wizard of Oz Testing

How the method is applied

1. **Design Interface:** Create an interface that users will interact with, ensuring it looks operational.

2. **Select a 'Wizard':** Choose someone to manually respond to user actions behind the scenes.

3. **Define System Responses:** Establish a set of standardized responses for the 'wizard' to follow.

4. **Conduct the Test:** Users interact with the interface, believing it's automated, while the 'wizard' performs system operations manually.

5. **Gather User Feedback:** After the session, collect feedback on the system's perceived functionality, usability, and any potential improvements.

6. **Analyze and Iterate:** Use insights from the test to refine the system's design and functionality before actual development.

 IBM has used Wizard of Oz testing to simulate and test conversational AI interfaces before fully developing them.

Responsive Design Testing

How might we

Ensure a seamless user experience across diverse devices and screen sizes.

What you can do with the method...

Responsive Design Testing evaluates how a design adapts and functions across different devices, from desktops to mobile phones, ensuring a consistent and user-friendly experience. As users access content from various devices, it's vital that design elements, navigation, and overall functionality remain intuitive and aesthetically pleasing. This testing ensures that design fluidity and adaptability meet user expectations across all platforms.

Tip

Always test on real devices in addition to simulators. Physical device testing can reveal nuances and interactions often missed in virtual environments.

 Responsive design can increase mobile traffic by 20%, ensuring a seamless experience across devices. (Source: Google)

Responsive Design Testing

How the method is applied

1. **Identify Target Devices:** Determine the range of devices and screen sizes most commonly used by your target audience.

2. **Set Up Testing Environment:** Utilize device emulators/simulators and tools like browser resizing utilities to mimic various screens.

3. **Conduct Initial Review:** Navigate the design on different devices, observing layout, images, and interactive elements.

4. **Document Inconsistencies:** Note any design breaks, misaligned elements, or functionality issues encountered during the review.

5. **Implement Fixes:** Adjust design and code to rectify observed inconsistencies, ensuring fluidity and functionality.

6. **Re-test & Iterate:** After implementing changes, re-test the design on all target devices, repeating the loop until optimal responsiveness is achieved.

 The Guardian conducts responsive design testing to ensure its website provides a seamless experience across all devices.

Evaluate and Refine

Heuristic Evaluation

How might we

Systematically evaluate a product's usability against established principles.

What you can do with the method...

Heuristic Evaluation is a usability inspection method where experts review a product or interface against predefined usability heuristics or principles. These heuristics, often seen as best practices, act as guidelines to pinpoint usability issues. By identifying areas where the product deviates from these principles, you can highlight potential pain points for users, ensuring that design changes prioritize enhanced user experience and satisfaction.

Tip

While Heuristic Evaluation reveals many usability issues, complement it with user testing. This combination offers a holistic view, merging expert insights with real user experiences.

 Heuristic evaluations can identify up to 75% of usability issues in a product. (Source: Nielsen Norman Group)

Heuristic Evaluation

How the method is applied

1. **Define Scope:** Clearly outline the areas of the product or interface to evaluate.

2. **Select Evaluators:** Engage 3-5 usability experts, ensuring a mix of perspectives for a comprehensive review.

3. **Brief on Heuristics:** Provide evaluators with a list of usability heuristics to guide their assessment. Nielsen's 10 heuristics are commonly used.

4. **Conduct Evaluation:** Experts independently navigate the product, noting areas that violate the heuristics and potential usability concerns.

5. **Compile Findings:** Consolidate observations from all evaluators, categorizing and prioritizing issues based on severity.

6. **Discuss & Plan:** Hold a debrief session to discuss findings. Create an actionable roadmap to address identified usability issues, ensuring design iterations focus on enhancing user experience.

 10 heuristics - Visibility of System Status, Match Between the System and the Real World, User Control and Freedom, Consistency and Standards, Error Prevention, Recognition Rather than Recall, Flexibility and Efficiency of Use, Aesthetic and Minimalist Design, Help Users Recognize, Diagnose, and Recover from Errors, Help and Documentation

Evaluate and Refine

Cognitive Walkthrough

How might we

Evaluate how intuitive and user-friendly a product is by simulating a user's problem-solving process.

What you can do with the method...

Cognitive Walkthrough enables you to assess an interface through the lens of a first-time user. By asking a series of questions like "Will the user know what to do?" or "Will the user see the result?", you get actionable insights into the user's journey. This technique is particularly useful in identifying design flaws or usability issues that may not be evident through other methods of evaluation.

Tip

For effective Cognitive Walkthroughs, involve a diverse team, including UX designers, developers, and even customer support. Different perspectives can uncover hidden pain points. It's also beneficial to conduct this exercise on competitor products to gain a comparative understanding.

 Usability testing with a cognitive walkthrough can identify 80% of usability problems (Nielsen Norman Group)

Cognitive Walkthrough

How the method is applied

1. **Define User Goals:** Start by listing the tasks a user is likely to perform.

2. **Create Task Scenarios:** For each goal, create a realistic scenario that a user would follow.

3. **Perform Walkthrough:** Simulate the journey, asking a series of questions at each interaction point. Note any struggles or hurdles.

4. **Document Findings:** Record observations, paying particular attention to areas where the user might get stuck or feel confused.

5. **Analyze:** Discuss findings within the team, and categorize them into issues that need immediate attention, those that are moderate concerns, and those that are low-priority.

6. **Iterate:** Make necessary design changes based on the findings.

7. **Retest:** Once the design changes are made, re-run the Cognitive Walkthrough to validate that the identified issues have been adequately addressed.

 A cognitive walkthrough of a mobile banking app revealed that users struggled to find the option to set up a recurring transfer, leading to design changes that improved the discoverability and clarity of this feature.

Usability Checklist

How might we

Have a structured list ensuring all usability aspects of a design are thoroughly reviewed.

What you can do with the method...

A Usability Checklist provides a comprehensive list of factors and elements to consider when evaluating a design's user-friendliness. It ensures that common pitfalls and oversights are avoided, and every facet of the user experience is addressed. By systematically going through this list, designers can catch issues before they reach users, optimizing the interface for ease of use, efficiency, and overall satisfaction.

Tip

While a checklist is comprehensive, it's not exhaustive. Always complement it with user testing to capture nuances and contextual insights that a list might miss.

 Using a usability checklist can improve product usability by 30% by ensuring all key aspects are covered. (Source: Usability.gov)

Usability Checklist

How the method is applied

1. **Prepare the Checklist:** Develop a checklist tailored to your project, incorporating general usability principles and specific project requirements.

2. **Review Design Systematically:** Begin with broader categories, such as navigation, and move to detailed elements like button sizes.

3. **Cross-Reference with Standards:** Ensure your design aligns with established usability and accessibility guidelines.

4. **Engage Multiple Reviewers:** Different perspectives can catch varied issues, so involve multiple team members in the review process.

5. **Document Findings:** As you go through the list, note down areas that meet criteria and those that need improvement.

6. **Prioritize & Iterate:** Based on findings, prioritize areas of concern and make necessary design modifications. Regularly update and refine the checklist based on evolving usability understanding and standards.

 Gov.uk uses a usability checklist to ensure its digital services meet high standards of usability and accessibility.

Evaluate and Refine

In-person Observations

How might we

Directly observe users in their natural environment for genuine, unfiltered insights.

What you can do with the method...

In-person observations offer a firsthand look at how users interact with a product or service in their real-world settings. This method reveals contextual nuances, such as environmental or social factors, that might influence user behaviour. By observing without intervening, designers can capture spontaneous reactions, uncovering deep-rooted needs, pain points, and habits that might not emerge in controlled testing environments.

Tip

Stay unobtrusive and neutral. Your presence shouldn't influence the user's behavior. Take detailed notes, but also be mindful of non-verbal cues—body language can provide as much insight as verbal feedback. Always remember to respect privacy and obtain consent before any observation session.

 In-person observations can uncover 30% more usability issues compared to remote testing. (Source: Nielsen Norman Group)

Evaluate and Refine

In-person Observations

How the method is applied

1. **Determine Objectives:** Clearly outline what you hope to learn. Are you studying a specific behavior, environment, or broader user experience?

2. **Recruit Participants:** Choose individuals who represent your target user group. Ensure they're aware they'll be observed.

3. **Setup Observation:** Choose a suitable location where users naturally interact with the product or service. Ensure minimal disturbance.

4. **Observe Silently:** Stay in the background, avoiding any influence on the participant's behavior. Use tools like notepads or voice recorders to capture observations.

5. **Capture Context:** Note environmental factors, social interactions, or any external influences that might affect user behavior.

6. **Analyze & Synthesize:** Review your notes, identifying patterns, and key takeaways. Combine this with other research methods to form a comprehensive understanding.

 IKEA conducts in-person observations in its stores to understand how customers navigate and interact with its products.

Remote Usability Tests

How might we

Evaluate product usability with users, irrespective of geographical location, using digital tools.

What you can do with the method...

Remote Usability Tests allow designers to gauge product usability without physical presence, bridging distances efficiently. By leveraging video conferencing tools and screen sharing, you can observe users as they navigate your product, collecting invaluable insights. Especially in a world where remote work and collaboration are prevalent, this method ensures uninterrupted user feedback, thus making iterations based on real-world use.

Tip

Always ensure that users are comfortable with the technology being used. Before starting, run a brief tech-check to avoid hitches during the test. Keep the process interactive; the more natural the environment, the more genuine the feedback. Remember, it's about understanding their experience, not just ticking off tasks.

 Remote usability testing can reduce testing costs by 50% while providing valuable user insights. (Source: UserTesting)

Remote Usability Tests

How the method is applied

1. **Set Clear Objectives:** Understand what you aim to achieve. Are you testing a specific feature or overall usability?

2. **Choose the Right Tools:** Use reliable video conferencing and screen sharing tools that users are comfortable with.

3. **Participant Selection:** Recruit users that fit your target demographic. Ensure they have a stable internet connection.

4. **Pre-test Run:** Before the main test, run a short session to familiarize users with the tools and process. This reduces anxiety and tech glitches.

5. **Conduct the Test:** Allow users to navigate the product, prompting them with tasks. Observe and note their interactions, struggles, and feedback.

6. **Analysis & Iteration:** Post-test, analyze the data. Look for patterns in user behavior, areas of struggle, and points of delight. Use these insights to refine your design.

 Dropbox conducts remote usability tests to gather feedback from users around the world and improve its products.

Eye Tracking

How might we

Understand where users focus on a screen, revealing patterns in visual attention.

What you can do with the method...

Eye tracking provides insights into where users look, for how long, and in what sequence. It's particularly valuable for evaluating UI clarity, ad effectiveness, or content hierarchy. By visualizing gaze paths and heatmaps, designers can discern which elements capture attention and which get overlooked. This tool is indispensable for refining designs to align with natural viewing patterns, ensuring vital information isn't missed.

Tip

Ensure the testing environment mimics real-world conditions. Brightness, distance, and screen size can affect results. Interpret data alongside other UX methods; while eye movement reveals 'where' and 'how long', it doesn't always explain 'why'.

 Eye tracking can provide 60% more insights into user behavior compared to traditional usability testing. (Source: NN Group)

Eye Tracking

How the method is applied

1. **Setup Equipment:** Ensure the eye-tracking device is calibrated correctly. Test it beforehand to ensure accuracy.

2. **Define Objectives:** Understand what you aim to uncover. Are you assessing a layout, ad, or another visual element?

3. **Select Participants:** Recruit users representing your target audience. Brief them on the process to make them comfortable.

4. **Conduct Sessions:** Allow participants to interact with the design. Monitor their eye movements in real-time.

5. **Analyze Heatmaps:** Post-session, generate heatmaps to visualize areas with the most and least attention.

6. **Interpret Gaze Plots:** Review the sequential path of visual attention. This shows the order in which elements are viewed.

 Walmart uses eye tracking to optimize the layout and design of its e-commerce website and improve product discoverability.

Evaluate and Refine

Heatmaps

How might we

Visually represent and analyze where users most frequently interact on a webpage or application.

What you can do with the method...

Heatmaps are visual representations of data, showing where users click, move, or hover on a page. The color-coded system, usually ranging from cool to hot, indicates areas of varying activity. They are instrumental in understanding user behavior, allowing designers to optimize layouts, CTA placements, and overall UX. By revealing 'hotspots', heatmaps guide towards design improvements, ensuring content aligns with user interests.

Tip

Always analyze heatmaps in context. High activity in an area doesn't always signify success; it could indicate confusion. Combine with other tools, like session replays, for a holistic view.

 Heatmaps can increase conversion rates by 20% by identifying areas of high user engagement. (Source: Crazy Egg)

Heatmaps

How the method is applied

1. **Define Objectives:** Understand what you're aiming to discover, be it engagement zones or potential pain points.

2. **Integrate Tool:** Use tools like Hotjar or Crazy Egg to integrate heatmap tracking on your site.

3. **Gather Data:** Allow users to interact with your page naturally over a period of time, ensuring a substantial amount of data.

4. **Review Heat Patterns:** Analyze 'hot' and 'cold' zones to see where users interact the most and least.

5. **Cross-reference Data:** Use scroll maps and click maps in conjunction to get a clearer picture of user behavior.

6. **Iterate Design:** Based on findings, make necessary design adjustments to enhance user experience and engagement.

 Booking.com uses heatmaps to understand how users interact with its website and identify areas for improvement.

Analytics Monitoring

How might we

Track, measure, and analyze user interactions and behaviors within a digital product.

What you can do with the method...

Analytics Monitoring provides insights into user behavior, demographics, and engagement metrics. By tracking user interactions, you can identify patterns, drop-offs, and successful pathways. This data-driven approach informs UX/UI decisions, leading to optimized user journeys, increased conversions, and enhanced user experiences. Beyond user behavior, it offers a peek into technical performance, like page load times and device usage.

Tip

Avoid 'paralysis by analysis'. While data is valuable, focus on key metrics that align with your goals. Over-reliance can hinder intuition and creativity.

 Companies that use analytics monitoring are 5 times more likely to make faster decisions. (Source: Bain & Company)

Analytics Monitoring

How the method is applied

1. **Define Goals:** Establish clear objectives for what you aim to achieve with analytics, be it improved conversions, user retention, or engagement.

2. **Choose a Platform:** Utilize platforms like Google Analytics, Mixpanel, or Adobe Analytics to implement tracking on your site.

3. **Implement Tracking Codes:** Embed the necessary tracking scripts or tags on your website or application to capture user data.

4. **Monitor Real-Time Data:** Observe user interactions, traffic sources, and activity as they happen in real-time.

5. **Analyze Trends:** Over time, identify trends, peaks, or drops in user behavior, helping to pinpoint areas of interest or concern.

6. **Iterate Based on Insights:** Use the insights gathered to inform design changes, content adjustments, and strategic shifts.

 Google uses Google Analytics to monitor user behavior and gain insights to improve its products and services.

Customer Satisfaction Score

How might we

Quickly gauge the satisfaction level of customers after specific interactions.

What you can do with the method...

CSAT (Customer Satisfaction Score) is a straightforward metric that measures a customer's satisfaction with a specific experience, product, or service. By asking questions like "How satisfied were you with your experience?", customers typically rate on a scale, often from 1 (very unsatisfied) to 5 (very satisfied). The average score gives a snapshot of overall satisfaction, making it a handy tool for real-time feedback.

Tip

While CSAT captures immediate feedback, it may not reflect long-term satisfaction or loyalty. Use CSAT alongside other metrics for a comprehensive view.

 A 5% increase in customer satisfaction can lead to a 25% to 95% increase in profits. (Source: Bain & Company)

Customer Satisfaction Score

How the method is applied

1. **Determine Touchpoints:** Identify crucial interaction points where you want to gauge satisfaction, e.g., post-purchase, after support calls.

2. **Craft the Survey:** Develop a concise survey with a clear question about the satisfaction level.

3. **Deploy the Survey:** Share the survey via email, on-site pop-ups, or within mobile apps, immediately post-interaction.

4. **Gather Responses:** Collect customer ratings over a set period or after a specific number of interactions.

5. **Calculate CSAT Score:** Sum up all scores and divide by the total number of respondents. Multiply by 20 to convert to a percentage.

6. **Analyze and Act:** Break down scores by demographics or touchpoints. Use open feedback to pinpoint areas of improvement.

 Amazon closely monitors its Customer Satisfaction Score (CSAT) to gauge customer sentiment and identify areas for improvement.

Net Promoter Score

How might we

Gauge customer loyalty and satisfaction using a simple metric.

What you can do with the method...

NPS (Net Promoter Score) is a powerful tool to measure customer loyalty by asking a single question: "On a scale of 0-10, how likely are you to recommend our product/service to a friend or colleague?" Based on responses, customers are categorized as Promoters (9-10), Passives (7-8), and Detractors (0-6). The NPS score is then derived by subtracting the percentage of Detractors from the percentage of promoters.

Tip

While NPS provides a snapshot of loyalty, dive deeper into feedback for actionable insights. Always seek the 'why' behind scores. NPS can be a game-changer, offering valuable insights into customer loyalty and areas needing attention.

 Companies with high Net Promoter Scores grow at more than twice the rate of their competitors. (Source: Bain & Company)

Net Promoter Score

How the method is applied

1. **Survey Creation:** Develop a simple survey with the core NPS question and an optional open-ended question for feedback.

2. **Timing is Key:** Decide the optimal time to administer the survey, with post-purchase or post-interaction being common choices.

3. **Collect Responses:** Use various channels like emails, apps, or websites to reach out to a diverse range of customers.

4. **Categorize Respondents:** Based on scores, label respondents as Promoters, Passives, or Detractors.

5. **Calculate NPS:** Subtract the percentage of Detractors from the percentage of Promoters. The score will range from -100 to 100.

6. **Analyze Feedback:** Beyond the score, analyze open-ended feedback to uncover reasons behind scores and identify areas of improvement.

 Apple closely monitors its Net Promoter Score (NPS) to gauge customer loyalty and identify opportunities for improvement.

System Usability Scale

How might we

Assess the usability of a product through a reliable, standardized survey method.

What you can do with the method...

SUS (System Usability Scale) is a quick and widely recognized tool to gauge the perceived usability of your product. It comprises 10 standard questions, providing a broad view of subjective usability assessments. Its scale, ranging from 0 to 100, doesn't represent a percentage but offers an indicative measure of your product's usability and the potential areas for improvement.

Tip

Remember, SUS gives a high-level view of usability. While scores below 68 might indicate usability issues, always combine SUS with other detailed usability methods for comprehensive insights.

 The System Usability Scale (SUS) is a reliable tool for measuring usability, with a score above 68 considered above average. (Source: Usability.gov)

System Usability Scale

How the method is applied

1. **Determine Timing:** Decide when to administer the SUS, usually after usability testing or at product milestones.

2. **Administer the Survey:** Present the 10 standard SUS questions to participants. Ensure they answer each question based on their feelings, not overthinking.

3. **Calculate the Score:** For odd items, subtract one from the user response. For even items, subtract the user responses from 5. Sum all scores and multiply by 2.5.

4. **Interpret the Results:** Though SUS scores aren't percentages, a score above 68 is considered above average, and below it may indicate usability issues.

5. **Combine with Other Methods:** Use the SUS in conjunction with in-depth usability testing methods to gain a holistic understanding.

6. **Iterate and Reassess:** Make design changes based on feedback and retest using SUS to monitor improvements in usability. **Objective Setting:** Clearly define what you aim to und

 Microsoft uses the System Usability Scale (SUS) to measure the usability of its products and identify areas for improvement.

Time-on-task Measurement

How might we

Understand how long users spend on specific tasks within my digital product or website.

What you can do with the method...

Time-on-Task Measurement provides insights into how much time users take to complete a specific task. This metric can reveal usability issues, such as overly complicated processes or unclear instructions. Shorter times might indicate efficiency, while longer times might point to challenges or confusion, aiding in optimizing user experience.

Tip

An optimized task shouldn't just be quick but intuitive. Sometimes, a longer time-on-task indicates deeper engagement, not just difficulty.

 Reducing time-on-task by 20% can significantly improve user satisfaction and productivity. (Source: Nielsen Norman Group)

Time-on-task Measurement

How the method is applied

1. **Define Tasks:** Clearly identify tasks you want to measure. This could range from sign-ups, checkouts, or using a particular feature.

2. **Tools:** Utilize analytics tools capable of tracking user interactions and time spent on tasks.

3. **Monitor Baseline:** Before making changes, record the average time users spend on the task for a baseline measurement.

4. **Identify Outliers:** Look for exceptionally short or long task durations. Understand the reasons behind these outliers.

5. **Implement Changes:** Based on findings, refine task processes, simplify workflows, or provide clearer instructions.

6. **Analyze & Iterate:** After changes, compare the new time-on-task to the baseline. Repeat the process to continuously optimize.

> LinkedIn measures time-on-task to understand how efficiently users can complete key tasks on its platform.

Error Rate Measurement

How might we

Monitor and reduce the number of errors users encounter while interacting with a system.

What you can do with the method...

Error Rate Management is about measuring the frequency of errors that users encounter and implementing strategies to reduce them. High error rates can frustrate users, leading to reduced satisfaction and potential abandonment. Monitoring these errors provides insights into system flaws, user misunderstandings, or areas needing better user guidance.

Tip

Errors aren't just system faults. They can signify usability issues. Addressing the root cause, not just the symptom, ensures a smoother user experience.

 Reducing error rates by 10% can improve user satisfaction by 20%. (Source: Usability.gov)

Error Rate Measurement

How the method is applied

1. **Track Errors:** Use analytics tools to monitor and log user-generated errors in real-time.

2. **Categorize Errors:** Group errors by type, frequency, and severity to prioritize fixes.

3. **Analyze User Paths:** Determine the common paths leading to errors. Identify if specific user segments are more prone to certain errors.

4. **Implement Fixes:** Address the most frequent and severe errors first. This might involve system improvements or clearer user guidance.

5. **Educate Users:** Sometimes, errors arise from misunderstandings. Offer tooltips, help guides, or tutorials to guide users.

6. **Re-Evaluate:** After implementing changes, monitor error rates to gauge the effectiveness of your interventions.

 Airbnb measures error rates to identify and fix issues that negatively impact the user experience.

Execute and Launch

In this phase, the validated designs are seamlessly integrated into the development process, ensuring a smooth and successful launch of the solution.

1. Agile Development
2. DevOps Pipeline Integration
3. Pair Designing
4. User Acceptance Testing (UAT)
5. Version Control
6. Design Handoff
7. Component Library
8. QA Testing

Execute and Launch

Agile Development

How might we

Implement a flexible and iterative approach for faster product delivery and continuous improvement.

What you can do with the method...

Agile Development promotes adaptive planning, timely delivery, and a flexible response to change. It breaks down projects into manageable units, prioritizes tasks, and allows teams to deliver high-quality software faster and with better alignment to user needs. Iterative cycles, or 'sprints', ensure regular feedback and refinement.

Tip

Always maintain open communication. Regularly review and adapt based on feedback, ensuring the team remains aligned with the project's goals and user needs.

 Agile development can increase project success rates by 28% compared to traditional methods. (Source: Project Management Institute)

Agile Development

How the method is applied

1. **Product Backlog Creation:** List all features, functionalities, and requirements. Prioritize them based on business and user needs.

2. **Sprint Planning:** Decide on the scope of the next sprint (usually 2–4 weeks). Select items from the backlog to be addressed.

3. **Daily Stand-ups:** Short meetings where the team discusses what was done the previous day, plans for the current day, and identifies any blockers.

4. **Sprint Review:** At the end of each sprint, review the work completed and demonstrate it to stakeholders.

5. **Retrospective:** Reflect on the past sprint. Identify what went well, what could be improved, and plan actions for the next sprint.

6. **Iterate:** Start the next sprint cycle. Over time, continuously refine and reprioritize the product backlog based on feedback and new insights.

> Spotify uses Agile development methodologies to quickly iterate and deliver new features based on user feedback.

DevOps Pipeline Integration

How might we

Integrate design seamlessly into the DevOps process, ensuring design continuity and efficiency.

What you can do with the method...

DevOps Pipeline Integration bridges the gap between development, operations, and design. For a designer, it means that design assets, feedback, and iterations can be seamlessly incorporated into the development cycle. This integration streamlines the process, ensuring that designs are consistently updated, tested, and deployed, resulting in a cohesive user experience and faster product releases.

Tip

For designers, understanding the DevOps workflow is crucial. Engage with the development team early and often. Use tools that offer design versioning and compatibility with DevOps tools. This ensures that design changes align with development sprints and releases.

 Integrating UX into the DevOps pipeline can improve product quality and user satisfaction by 20%. (Source: DevOps Institute)

DevOps Pipeline Integration

How the method is applied

1. **Familiarization:** Understand the DevOps stages and pinpoint where design integration occurs.

2. **Open Communication:** Maintain a dialogue with developers and operations teams to ensure alignment.

3. **Seamless Integration:** Choose design tools compatible with the DevOps tools for smooth integration and collaboration.

4. **Automated Design Checks:** Implement tests within the pipeline to validate design consistency and user experience.

5. **Rapid Feedback:** Establish a system for immediate feedback on design iterations to address user needs quickly.

6. **Consistent Updates:** Ensure all design modifications are part of the continuous deployment, keeping the product's design current.

 Netflix has fully integrated UX design into its DevOps pipeline to ensure fast and efficient delivery of new features.

Execute and Launch

Pair Designing

How might we

Harness the collaborative power of two designers working in tandem for superior design outcomes.

What you can do with the method...

Pair designing involves two designers collaboratively working on the same design task. It merges their unique perspectives, enhancing creativity and problem-solving. This approach reduces design blind spots, accelerates decision-making, and fosters knowledge sharing. Whether brainstorming, wireframing, or refining UI details, the collaborative synergy often leads to richer and more holistic design solutions.

Tip

Maintain open communication and be receptive to feedback. Use this method to balance strengths and weaknesses, ensuring the design remains user-centric and efficient.

 Pair designing can increase design efficiency and creativity by 30% by fostering collaboration. (Source: Interaction Design Foundation)

Pair Designing

How the method is applied

1. **Define Roles:** Start by designating one designer as the 'driver' (the one actively designing) and the other as the 'navigator' (offering insights, suggestions, and critiques).

2. **Brainstorm Together:** Initiate the design process with a joint brainstorming session, discussing ideas and gathering diverse viewpoints.

3. **Collaborative Sketching:** Sketch ideas collaboratively, allowing both designers to input and iterate on concepts.

4. **Rapid Prototyping:** Using a design tool, the driver translates ideas into prototypes, while the navigator provides continuous feedback.

5. **Review & Reflect:** Regularly pause to evaluate the design's direction, ensuring alignment with user needs and design principles.

6. **Switch Roles:** Periodically swap roles to infuse fresh perspectives and balance the workload.

 Airbnb has used pair designing to foster collaboration and knowledge sharing among its design team.

Execute and Launch

User Acceptance Testing (UAT)

How might we

Ensure designs align with user expectations, meeting both functionality and usability criteria.

What you can do with the method...

User Acceptance Testing (UAT) is the final phase of testing where real users interact with the software or product to validate its design against business objectives. From a designer's perspective, it offers insights into the user experience, highlighting areas for improvement. UAT provides a critical checkpoint before the launch, ensuring designs meet actual user needs and expectations, enhancing overall satisfaction.

Tip

For designers, UAT is less about code and more about experience. Engage a diverse user base for testing to capture a wide spectrum of feedback. This richness in perspective can lead to designs that resonate more broadly and deeply with your target audience.

 User acceptance testing can increase user satisfaction by 20% by ensuring the product meets user needs and expectations. (Source: Project Management Institute)

User Acceptance Testing (UAT)

How the method is applied

1. **Objective Definition:** Clearly specify what you expect from the design in terms of user experience and functionality.

2. **Test Planning:** Identify a diverse group of users and set the test environment, ensuring it mimics real-world usage.

3. **Scenario Creation:** Outline real-world tasks that users might perform. This provides tangible actions to evaluate.

4. **Execution:** Users interact with the design, completing specified tasks while their experience is closely monitored.

5. **Feedback Collection:** Gather user opinions, feelings, and suggestions. This qualitative data is pivotal for refining designs.

6. **Analysis & Iteration:** Review feedback, identify patterns, and adjust designs accordingly. Repeat testing if necessary until user satisfaction is attained.

 The UK Government Digital Service conducts user acceptance testing to ensure its digital services meet the needs of citizens.

Version Control

How might we

Understand the significance and application of version control in design and development realms.

What you can do with the method...

Version Control is a system that records changes to files over time, enabling one to revert to specific versions later. It's crucial in design and development as it tracks revisions, prevents data loss, and fosters team collaboration. Designers and developers can work simultaneously without overwriting each other's contributions, ensuring an organized workflow. It's a safeguard against mistakes, allowing teams to review, compare, and restore previous versions.

Tip

Use clear naming for version history to prevent confusion. Commit changes often with concise messages for easy tracking. Sync with the central repository regularly. Employ branching for experimental tasks and merge once they've been tested and are stable.

 Using version control can reduce development errors by 30% by ensuring proper tracking and management of changes. (Source: GitHub)

Version Control

How the method is applied

1. **Set Up Repository:** Begin by setting up a central repository. This will be the main hub where all versions are stored.

2. **Clone Repository:** Each contributor creates a 'clone' of this repository on their local machine, ensuring they have the latest version.

3. **Make Changes:** Designers or developers work on their tasks, making modifications to their local files.

4. **Commit Changes:** After completing a task or reaching a milestone, changes are 'committed' with a descriptive message detailing the update.

5. **Push to Central:** The committed changes are then 'pushed' to the central repository. This updates the main version with the recent changes.

6. **Resolve Conflicts:** If multiple contributors make conflicting changes, the system will flag it. Team members must then resolve the conflict before the changes are merged.

 Facebook uses version control to manage and track changes to its codebase and design assets.

Design Handoff

How might we

Seamlessly transition design concepts to development teams without losing design intent.

What you can do with the method...

Design handoff bridges the gap between designers and developers. It involves providing developers with a complete, functional visual representation of the design, along with assets, specs, and code snippets. This ensures designs are implemented accurately, maintaining the design's integrity and vision.

Tip

Ensure that both the design and development teams are aligned from the start. Regular communication and collaborative tools can prevent common handoff issues.

 Effective design handoff can reduce development time by 30% by ensuring clear communication and alignment. (Source: Zeplin)

Design Handoff

How the method is applied

1. **Documentation:** Begin with comprehensive documentation. Detail the design's rationale, interactions, and animations.

2. **Select Tools:** Use handoff tools like Zeplin, Figma, or Sketch that can provide exact specifications, assets, and even code suggestions.

3. **Review Designs:** Before the handoff, conduct a review with developers. Address queries and provide clarifications on design choices.

4. **Provide Assets:** Ensure all assets—icons, images, fonts— are available in the required formats and resolutions.

5. **Stay Available:** Post-handoff, be accessible for questions or clarifications. Sometimes, design nuances might need further explanation.

6. **Feedback Loop:** Encourage developers to provide feedback on the design. This can be invaluable for future projects and understanding practical implementation challenges.

 InVision has developed tools to streamline the design handoff process and ensure smooth collaboration between design and development teams.

Component Library

How might we

Leverage a centralized repository for maintaining design consistency and streamlining workflows.

What you can do with the method...

A Component Library acts as a curated collection of reusable UI elements. It ensures uniformity across different parts of a product, speeds up design processes, and fosters a seamless collaboration between designers and developers. By having a single source of truth for design components, teams can reduce design inconsistencies, thereby enhancing user experience.

Tip

Regularly update and document your Component Library. Collaborate with developers to ensure the components align with development practices. This synergy not only maintains design integrity but also eases the transition from design to code.

> Using a component library can reduce design and development time by 50%, leading to faster product releases. (Source: InVision)

Execute and Launch

Component Library

How the method is applied

1. **Purpose Definition:** Ascertain the project's scope and identify frequently utilized components.

2. **Categorize:** Group components by their functionality, such as 'Inputs' or 'Overlays'.

3. **Design & Detail:** Craft each component according to brand standards. Include guidelines for usage and potential variations.

4. **Developer Sync:** Engage with developers to ensure the components are practical for coding. Tools like Figma or Sketch can be handy for this collaboration.

5. **Manage Versions:** Maintain different versions of your library, enabling reversions if necessary.

6. **Routine Check:** Schedule reviews of the library, phasing out old components, and introducing contemporary designs.

7. **Tool Integration:** Embed the library within design tools for easy accessibility, ensuring uniformity across projects.

 IBM has developed a comprehensive component library, the IBM Carbon Design System, to ensure consistency and efficiency in its product development.

Execute and Launch

QA Testing

How might we

Ensure design integrity and functionality before a product's public release.

What you can do with the method...

QA Testing is an essential step in the design-to-deployment journey. Through meticulous examination, designers validate that the implemented designs mirror their original concepts. Beyond just aesthetics, QA Testing assesses interactions, transitions, and usability, ensuring a flawless user experience. By preemptively detecting discrepancies or issues, designers can guarantee that end-users interact with a product that's both visually cohesive and functionally robust.

Tip

Incorporate real users in your QA process. Their interactions and feedback can unearth nuances and provide insights that might be overlooked in a purely technical evaluation. Authentic user experiences lead to more actionable feedback.

 Effective QA testing can reduce post-release defects by 50%, ensuring a smoother user experience. (Source: Project Management Institute)

QA Testing

How the method is applied

1. **Criteria Setting:** Define product standards and desired outcomes, laying a foundation for effective testing.

2. **Scenario Execution:** Design diverse test scenarios. In controlled settings, simulate real-world user behaviors to evaluate all design facets.

3. **Document & Refine:** Record test results, especially design glitches or inconsistencies. Modify design based on findings.

4. **User Testing:** Engage real users for genuine feedback. Their interactions can pinpoint areas of improvement in design.

5. **Final Review:** Post-refinement, conduct an exhaustive check, ensuring the design adheres to all standards and offers a user-friendly experience.

 Microsoft conducts extensive QA testing to ensure its products are high-quality and bug-free before release.

Analyze and Enhance

This phase involves continuous monitoring of the launched solution, analyzing user behavior and performance metrics, and implementing data-driven enhancements.

1. AI-led Personalized Experiences
2. Predictive User Feedback
3. Churn Rate Analysis
4. Cohort Analysis
5. Conversion Funnel Analysis
6. Feedback Surveys
7. Field Survey
8. Iterative Testing
9. Lifetime Value Analysis
10. Longitudinal Study
11. Performance Metrics
12. User Analytics

AI-led Personalized Experiences

How might we

leverage AI and machine learning to analyze user data and anticipate user needs, preferences, and behaviors, enabling us to create proactive and intuitive user experiences that meet users' expectations?

What you can do with the method...

AI-led personalized experiences involve using artificial intelligence to analyze individual user data and tailor the user interface, content, and interactions accordingly. By leveraging AI's ability to process vast amounts of user data, designers can create highly customized experiences that resonate with each user, ultimately enhancing user satisfaction and loyalty.

Tip

Utilize AI's ability to process vast amounts of user data to create highly customized experiences that cater to individual users' preferences, behaviors, and contexts. This personalized approach can significantly enhance user engagement and satisfaction.

 80% of customers are more likely to buy from a company that provides personalized experiences (McKinsey & Company)

AI-led Personalized Experiences

How the method is applied

1. **Data Collection:** Gather data on user behavior, preferences, and interactions across various touchpoints. Use this data to build detailed user profiles.

2. **AI Integration:** Implement AI algorithms to analyze the collected data and identify patterns and preferences. Use machine learning models to predict user needs and behaviors.

3. **Personalized Content:** Use AI to dynamically generate and present personalized content, such as product recommendations, personalized messages, and tailored user interfaces.

4. **Testing and Optimization:** Continuously test the AI-generated personalized experiences with real users. Gather feedback and use it to optimize the algorithms and improve the accuracy and relevance of the personalization.

5. **Continuous Learning:** Implement a system for continuous learning where the AI adapts to new data and evolving user preferences. Regularly update the AI models to ensure they stay relevant and effective in delivering personalized experiences.

 Spotify employs AI-led personalization to curate unique playlists and music recommendations for each user based on their listening history, preferences, and context, creating a highly engaging and personalized music streaming experience.

Predictive User Feedback

How might we

Leverage AI and machine learning algorithms to analyze user data and anticipate user needs, preferences, and behaviors. This proactive approach can help designers create more user-centric experiences that meet users' expectations.

What you can do with the method...

Predictive user feedback utilizes AI and machine learning to analyze vast amounts of user data, enabling designers to forecast future user actions and provide proactive solutions. By predicting user behavior, preferences, and needs, designers can create interfaces that are not just reactive but proactive in meeting user expectations, ultimately enhancing the overall user experience.

Tip

To utilize AI's ability to process vast amounts of user data to create highly customized experiences that cater to individual users' preferences, behaviors, and contexts, ultimately enhancing user engagement and satisfaction?

 Companies using AI to personalize customer experiences see a 20% increase in sales (Forbes)

 Netflix leverages predictive feedback to analyze viewing habits, offering personalized content recommendations tailored to users' preferences.

Predictive User Feedback

How the method is applied

1. **Data Collection:** Gather relevant user data from various sources, such as user interactions, preferences, and feedback.

2. **Data Analysis:** Use AI and machine learning algorithms to analyze the collected data and identify patterns, trends, and correlations.

3. **Predictive Modeling:** Develop predictive models based on the analyzed data to forecast future user behaviors, preferences, and needs. Collaborate with researchers, product managers and technology teams.

4. **Proactive Design:** Incorporate predictive insights into the design process to create proactive and user-centric experiences that anticipate user needs.

5. **Continuous Improvement:** Regularly update and refine predictive models based on new user data and feedback to ensure the accuracy and relevance of the predictions.

6. **User Testing:** Validate the effectiveness of predictive user feedback through user testing and gather additional insights to further improve the user experience.

7. **Iteration:** Continuously iterate and refine the design based on user feedback and predictive insights to create a seamless and intuitive user experience.

Churn Rate Analysis

How might we

analyze user behavior and engagement patterns to identify factors contributing to user churn, enabling us to develop strategies to retain users and reduce churn rates?

What you can do with the method...

Churn Rate Analysis offers insights into user attrition over time. By assessing the percentage of users who cease using a service, designers gain clarity on potential design flaws or user pain points. This metric serves as a crucial feedback loop in UX/UI, enabling designers to detect issues, improve user satisfaction, and ensure a seamless user journey. It's a pivotal tool in refining user experience and ensuring long-term engagement.

Tip

High churn often hints at underlying user experience issues. Don't just analyze the numbers; delve deeper to understand user motivations and pain points. Combine churn rate findings with qualitative feedback for a holistic understanding. Regularly revisiting and analyzing this metric can guide iterative design improvements.

 Reducing churn by 5% can increase profitability by 25% to 95% (Harvard Business Review).

Churn Rate Analysis

How the method is applied

1. **Data Collection:** Start by gathering user data from analytics tools, identifying users who've stopped using the service.

2. **Calculate Churn Rate:** Use the formula: (Users at the start of the period - Users at the end of the period) / Users at the start of the period.

3. **Segment Analysis:** Break down the churn rate by user demographics, behaviors, or product features to identify specific problem areas.

4. **Qualitative Feedback:** Supplement quantitative data with qualitative insights. Conduct exit interviews or surveys to understand reasons behind user departures.

5. **Identify Patterns:** Analyze if users are leaving after specific interactions or during particular periods. This can pinpoint problematic areas in the design.

6. **Iterative Improvements:** Based on findings, make necessary design changes. Continuously monitor the churn rate post-adjustments to measure the impact of changes and further refine as needed.

 Netflix uses churn rate analysis to understand why users cancel their subscriptions. By analyzing viewing habits, feedback, and engagement data, Netflix can identify at-risk users and offer personalized content recommendations or special offers to retain them.

Cohort Analysis

How might we

Delve into user behaviors, segmenting by shared experiences to optimize design strategies.

What you can do with the method...

Cohort Analysis segments users based on shared characteristics or experiences within a defined time span. By observing these cohorts, designers can identify patterns and trends in user behavior. This can reveal how different groups interact with a product or how changes in design affect user engagement. It's a powerful tool to understand user retention, product adoption, and the effectiveness of design iterations over time.

Tip

When conducting Cohort Analysis, be specific in defining cohorts. It's not just about grouping users, but understanding why a particular group behaves a certain way. Dive deep into the data and ask questions. The richness of insights comes from the interplay between the cohorts and the events or experiences you're analyzing.

 Companies that use cohort analysis can improve user retention by up to 20% (Mixpanel).

Cohort Analysis

How the method is applied

1. **Segmentation:** Start by defining your cohorts based on shared attributes or experiences, like sign-up date or feature usage.

2. **Data Collection:** Gather data on user interactions, retention, and any other relevant metrics for each cohort.

3. **Analysis:** Compare cohorts against each other to identify trends, behaviors, or patterns that are unique to each segment.

4. **Visualization:** Use graphs and charts to visualize the data, making it easier to spot trends or anomalies among different cohorts.

5. **Interpretation:** Understand the 'why' behind the patterns. This might involve further research or user interviews to gain deeper insights.

6. **Implementation:** Use the insights gained to make informed design decisions, whether it's refining current features or introducing new ones.

> Airbnb uses cohort analysis to track the behavior of hosts and guests. By comparing cohorts based on their sign-up date, Airbnb can understand how changes in the platform affect user engagement and retention over time.

Conversion Funnel Analysis

How might we

Optimize user journeys, identify drop-offs, and boost overall conversion rates effectively.

What you can do with the method...

Conversion Funnel Analysis provides a visual representation of the user's journey from awareness to action. By assessing each stage of the funnel, designers can identify barriers or drop-off points, optimizing user flow and increasing conversion rates. This tool offers a holistic view of the user experience, allowing designers to pinpoint friction points and make data-driven design decisions to enhance user engagement and conversions.

Tip

Consistency is key. Ensure each stage of the funnel aligns with user expectations. Regularly reassess the funnel, especially after design changes. A minor alteration can significantly impact user flow. Dive deep into drop-off points, seeking qualitative feedback to understand the 'why' behind user actions.

 Optimizing the conversion funnel can increase conversion rates by up to 50% (Econsultancy).

Conversion Funnel Analysis

How the method is applied

1. **Define Stages:** Break down the user journey into distinct stages, from initial contact to the final action.

2. **Gather Data:** Use analytics tools to collect data on user behavior at each stage.

3. **Visualize Funnel:** Represent the journey visually, showcasing user numbers at each stage and the drop-off rates between stages.

4. **Identify Drop-offs:** Pinpoint stages with high attrition rates, indicating potential usability or design issues.

5. **Gather Feedback:** Engage users who exited the funnel prematurely through surveys or interviews to understand their reasons.

6. **Implement Changes:** Use insights from the analysis to refine design elements, CTAs, or content that may be hindering conversions.

7. **Reassess Regularly:** Continuously monitor the funnel, especially after design updates, to ensure optimized performance.

Amazon uses conversion funnel analysis to optimize its checkout process. By analyzing user behavior at each step, Amazon identifies friction points and implements changes, such as one-click purchasing, to streamline the process and increase conversion rates.

Feedback Surveys

How might we

Gather insights directly from users, enhancing future iterations of my product.

What you can do with the method...

Feedback Surveys are pivotal for designers seeking genuine user reactions. These tools unveil user sentiments, highlighting what's working and what's not in a design. They bridge the communication gap, providing a clear path for product enhancements. Through structured queries, designers can extract actionable insights, facilitating a more user-centric design approach, and fostering product evolution based on actual user needs.

Tip

Craft your surveys with brevity and clarity to encourage completion. Diversify your questions, balancing multiple-choice and open-ended ones for a holistic view. Remember, the true value of a survey lies not just in gathering feedback, but in effectively acting on the insights to enhance the user experience.

 Companies that actively collect and act on user feedback can increase customer satisfaction by up to 20% (Gartner).

Feedback Surveys

How the method is applied

1. **Objective Definition:** Begin by outlining what you hope to achieve. Is it understanding a new feature's reception or general user satisfaction?

2. **Question Design:** Create clear, unbiased questions. Include a mix of scales (like Likert), multiple choice, and open-ended queries.

3. **Pilot Test:** Before full distribution, test the survey on a small group to identify any confusing questions or technical glitches.

4. **Distribution:** Use email, in-app prompts, or social media to distribute the survey. Ensure you're reaching a diverse segment of your user base.

5. **Analysis:** Once responses are in, use statistical tools and qualitative analysis to interpret results. Look for patterns, outliers, and areas of concern or success.

6. **Implementation:** Use the insights to inform design iterations. Address pain points, validate successful design elements, and prioritize changes based on user feedback.

 RethinkingUX, a global design community and India's largest design community, uses feedback surveys to gather user insights on initiatives and overall satisfaction. By analyzing survey responses, RethinkingUX can prioritize feature updates and improvements that align with user needs.

Field Survey

How might we

Engage with the environment and context in which users operate to inform and inspire innovative design solutions that fit seamlessly into their lives.

What you can do with the method...

Field surveys allow you to collect observational and ethnographic data that reveals how users interact with products or services in real-world settings. This method can uncover details that users themselves might not be aware of, leading to more intuitive and user-centric design.

Tip

When conducting field surveys, immerse yourself in the user's environment to gather contextual data. Be observant and take note of environmental factors, user interactions, and behaviors. This hands-on approach provides a rich understanding of user needs and challenges in their natural setting.

 Field surveys can reveal up to 30% more usability issues compared to lab-based studies (Nielsen Norman Group).

Field Survey

How the method is applied

1. **Contextual Inquiry:** Initiate by observing users in their typical settings to understand their physical, social, and cultural contexts.

2. **Survey Design:** Formulate observational guidelines that capture user interactions, tasks, and responses to environmental factors.

3. **Pilot Test:** Conduct a preliminary field test to refine the survey approach, ensuring non-intrusive observation techniques.

4. **Execution:** Systematically observe, document, and gather data on user behaviors and environmental interactions using checklists and photos.

5. **Data Synthesis:** Analyze observations to identify behavioral patterns and insights using UX analysis tools like affinity diagrams.

6. **Insights Application:** Transform observations into actionable design enhancements, integrating discoveries into user personas, journey maps, and prototypes.

> Google conducts field surveys to understand how users interact with its products in different environments. By observing users in real-world settings, Google can gather contextual insights that inform product design and development.

Iterative Testing

How might we

Consistently refine designs based on real user feedback, ensuring optimal user experiences.

What you can do with the method...

Iterative testing isn't just about catching flaws; it's a strategic approach to design evolution. By integrating regular user feedback, designers can course-correct early, saving resources and time. Each iteration sharpens design focus, ensuring a product that resonates with its audience. Continuous feedback loops are key to achieving a user-centric solution.

Tip

Don't see iterative testing as a one-time fix but as a journey to perfection. Test rough sketches; early insights can prevent big redesigns. Embrace all feedback. It's your compass that guides design to user-centric excellence. Remember, iteration is the core of user-centered design.

 Iterative testing can reduce development costs by up to 50% by identifying issues early in the design process (Forrester Research).

Iterative Testing

How the method is applied

1. **Start Early:** Before diving deep into design details, test basic concepts or wireframes with a small user group.

2. **Identify Metrics:** Define what success looks like. It could be task completion rate, error rate, or user satisfaction scores.

3. **Conduct Tests:** Use various methods like usability testing, A/B tests, or first-click tests based on your design stage.

4. **Analyze Results:** Post-testing, gather all the data, and look for patterns. Are users consistently getting stuck at one step? Is a particular feature loved by all?

5. **Implement Changes:** Refine your design based on the feedback. This could mean changing a navigation structure, rewording a CTA, or redesigning a feature.

6. **Repeat:** After making changes, test the revised design with another group of users. Compare these results with previous tests to measure improvement.

 Adobe uses iterative testing to develop its software products. By continuously testing prototypes with users and incorporating feedback, Adobe ensures that its products are user-friendly and meet the needs of its diverse user base.

Analyze and Enhance

Lifetime Value Analysis

How might we

Grasp the long-term value of a user, optimizing retention and enhancing design profitability.

What you can do with the method...

Lifetime Value Analysis (LTV) quantifies the projected revenue a user will generate during their engagement with a product. By understanding LTV, designers can pinpoint the most valuable user segments, refine user experience to cater to these segments, and allocate resources effectively. It offers insights into the long-term impact of design decisions on profitability and helps prioritize features that drive higher user value.

Tip

LTV isn't just about revenue. Factor in user engagement, loyalty, and referrals. Higher LTV often indicates strong user-product fit and satisfaction. Regularly update your LTV calculations to reflect changing user behaviors and design modifications for accurate forecasting.

 Increasing customer retention rates by 5% can increase profits by 25% to 95% (Bain & Company).

Lifetime Value Analysis

How the method is applied

1. **Data Collection:** Gather data on user spend, frequency of interactions, and retention over time.

2. **Segmentation:** Categorize users based on demographics, behavior, or acquisition source.

3. **Calculation:** Use the formula: (Average Value of Sale) x (Number of Transactions) x (Retention Time Period) to compute LTV.

4. **Compare & Analyze:** Benchmark LTV against the cost of acquiring a user (CAC) to understand profitability. A higher LTV relative to CAC indicates a good return on investment.

5. **Feedback Integration:** Use LTV insights to identify areas of improvement in the design. High LTV segments might need more advanced features, while low LTV segments might indicate usability issues.

6. **Iterate & Optimize:** Continuously refine the product based on LTV insights, aiming to enhance the value provided to users, thereby increasing their LTV.

 Shopify uses lifetime value analysis to identify high-value merchants on its platform. By understanding the long-term value of these users, Shopify can develop targeted strategies to acquire and retain them, ultimately driving business growth.

Longitudinal Study

How might we

Deeply understand user behaviors and patterns over an extended period of time.

What you can do with the method...

Longitudinal studies offer insights into user behaviors, preferences, and challenges over time. Unlike one-off tests, they capture evolving user experiences, often revealing subtle shifts in behavior or satisfaction. By tracking users over weeks, months, or even years, designers can pinpoint design elements that remain effective and those that may need updates as user needs evolve.

Tip

Longitudinal studies excel in providing rich, context-heavy data. However, they demand patience and consistent monitoring. To maximize their benefits, ensure that data collection methods remain consistent throughout the study to capture accurate, comparable results.

 Longitudinal studies can provide deeper insights into user behavior and satisfaction compared to cross-sectional studies (Journal of User Experience).

Analyze and Enhance

Longitudinal Study

How the method is applied

1. **Objective Setting:** Define clear goals, focusing on specific user behaviors or long-term design efficacy.

2. **Participant Selection & Baseline Data:** Choose a diverse user group and gather initial data for future comparisons.

3. **Data Collection Methods:** Utilize tools and techniques such as surveys, interviews, or direct observations.

4. **Regular Monitoring & Analysis:** Set data collection intervals and analyze feedback after each phase to spot emerging patterns.

5. **Continuous Adjustments:** Based on interim findings, make necessary design tweaks to enhance user experience.

6. **Final Review:** At the conclusion, assess all data to uncover long-term trends and insights, shaping future design strategies.

 Facebook conducts longitudinal studies to track user engagement and satisfaction over time. By understanding how user behavior evolves, Facebook can make informed decisions about product updates and new features.

183

Performance Metrics

How might we

Gain insights into user experience and product efficiency through precise metrics analysis.

What you can do with the method...

Performance Metrics provide quantifiable data to evaluate a product's efficiency, responsiveness, and user satisfaction. These metrics help pinpoint bottlenecks, optimize load times, and ensure smooth user interactions. By tracking metrics such as page load times, server response times, and user engagement rates, designers can make informed decisions, enhancing the user experience and ensuring the product aligns with performance objectives.

Tip

Always align your performance metrics with your design and business goals. While it's essential to monitor standard metrics, it's equally vital to prioritize those directly influencing your users' experiences. Regularly reviewing and updating your metrics ensures you're always tuned into user needs and product efficiency.

 Companies that track performance metrics can improve product effectiveness by up to 30% (McKinsey & Company).

Performance Metrics

How the method is applied

1. **Goal Setting**: Define clear objectives for your design and select pertinent metrics like load times and engagement rates.

2. **Integration**: Use tools like Google Analytics to capture relevant data. Ensure seamless integration without performance hitches.

3. **Regular Monitoring**: Systematically review metrics to identify trends and anomalies that could impact user experience.

4. **Data Analysis**: Dive into metrics, understand user behaviors, and identify design areas causing inefficiencies.

5. **Iterative Changes**: Act on insights. Simplify content, optimize images, or make other changes to enhance performance.

6. **Review & Adapt**: Post-changes, revisit metrics to measure impact. Use new data to refine and continuously improve the design.

 Google Analytics provides a comprehensive set of performance metrics for website and app owners. By tracking metrics such as user engagement, conversion rates, and bounce rates, businesses can identify areas for improvement and optimize their digital

Analyze and Enhance

User Analytics

How might we

To harness data-driven insights to refine and optimize our design for superior user engagement.

What you can do with the method...

User Analytics provides a deep dive into how users interact with your design. It reveals engagement hotspots, navigation patterns, and pain points. By tracking metrics like bounce rate, session duration, and click-through rates, designers gain a window into user preferences and behaviors. This data not only identifies areas of friction but also guides iterative design improvements, ensuring alignment with user needs and maximizing engagement.

Tip

Leverage user analytics not as an end-point but as a continuous feedback loop. While numbers and graphs showcase user behavior, it's crucial to interpret this data contextually. Always correlate quantitative data with qualitative feedback for a holistic understanding, and iterate your design based on combined insights.

 Companies that use user analytics can improve user engagement by up to 25% (Forrester Research).

User Analytics

How the method is applied

1. **Setup & Integration:** Integrate tools like Google Analytics or Mixpanel into your platform for data collection.

2. **Define Metrics:** Pinpoint key performance indicators (KPIs) aligning with your design objectives.

3. **Data Harvesting:** Gather data over time, capturing varied user interactions for a holistic understanding.

4. **Insightful Analysis:** Delve into the data, spotlighting key trends and unexpected user behaviors.

5. **Feedback Synthesis:** Merge quantitative findings with qualitative user feedback for a well-rounded perspective.

6. **Iterative Refinement:** With the insights from analytics, modify the design to elevate user experience and rectify noted issues.

7. **Ongoing Monitoring:** After making changes, continuously monitor user interactions to assess the impact and be for more tweaks.

 Spotify uses user analytics to understand listening habits and preferences. By analyzing data on user interactions, Spotify can provide personalized music recommendations and create a more engaging user experience.

Evolve and Expand

In this phase, the insights gathered from monitoring and user feedback are used to drive iterative improvements, plan for scalability, and explore new opportunities for growth.

1. Design for Scalability
2. Design for Security
3. Scalability Testing
4. Design for Performance
5. Design for Accessibility
6. Design for Inclusivity
7. Design for User Engagement
8. Design for User Retention
9. Design for User Acquisition
10. Design for User Onboarding
11. Design for User Feedback
12. Gamification

Design for Scalability

How might we

Create products that can efficiently handle growth in users, features, and data without compromising performance or user experience.

What you can do with the method...

Designing for scalability involves creating systems and processes that can expand and evolve with the growing needs of your product. This means considering future growth and potential challenges from the outset, ensuring that your design can handle increased load, complexity, and data without major overhauls. Scalable design promotes long-term sustainability and adaptability.

Tip

Design with scalability in mind to ensure your product can grow and adapt without sacrificing performance or user experience. Scalable design solutions accommodate increasing users, data, and features seamlessly.

 83% of businesses say that scalability is a key factor in their long-term success. (Source: Deloitte)

Design for Scalability

How the method is applied

1. **Modular Design:** Create modular components that can be independently developed, tested, and updated. This approach allows for easy expansion and maintenance without disrupting the entire system.

2. **Flexible Architecture:** Design a flexible and robust architecture that can accommodate growth. Use scalable technologies and frameworks that support horizontal and vertical scaling.

3. **Performance Optimization:** Optimize for performance from the beginning. Ensure that your design can handle increased traffic and data without slowing down. Use efficient algorithms and data structures, and optimize load times and resource usage.

4. **Consistent Design Patterns:** Establish consistent design patterns and guidelines that promote scalability. This includes using responsive design principles, ensuring accessibility, and maintaining a cohesive visual language.

5. **Continuous Monitoring and Feedback:** Implement monitoring tools to track performance and user behavior. Regularly gather feedback from users and stakeholders to identify areas for improvement and ensure the design continues to meet scalability needs.

 AWS is a prime example of designing for scalability. AWS offers a range of cloud computing services that can scale up or down based on demand

Design for Security

How might we

Prioritize the security and privacy of user data in our designs, protecting against potential threats and vulnerabilities?

What you can do with the method...

Design for Security involves incorporating security measures and best practices throughout the design process to ensure that the system is protected against potential threats and vulnerabilities. This approach helps to minimize the risk of data breaches, unauthorized access, and other security incidents.

Tip

Implement a multi-layered security approach, including encryption, authentication, and authorization, to protect user data and prevent unauthorized access.

 60% of small businesses close within six months of a cyber attack, highlighting the importance of robust security design. (Source: National Cyber Security Alliance)

Design for Security

How the method is applied

1. **Threat Modeling:** Identify potential security threats and vulnerabilities early in the design process.

2. **Secure Architecture:** Design a secure system architecture that includes encryption, authentication, and authorization mechanisms.

3. **Secure Coding Practices:** Follow secure coding practices to prevent common vulnerabilities such as SQL injection and cross-site scripting (XSS).

4. **Security Testing:** Conduct regular security testing, including penetration testing and vulnerability scanning, to identify and address security issues.

5. **Incident Response Planning:** Develop an incident response plan to quickly detect, respond to, and recover from security incidents.

6. **Continuous Monitoring:** Continuously monitor the system for suspicious activity and potential security threats.

 The banking industry heavily invests in designing security measures to protect sensitive financial data and prevent unauthorized access to customer accounts.

Scalability Testing

How might we

Ensure that our designs can accommodate growth and increased usage without compromising performance or user experience?

What you can do with the method...

Scalability Testing involves testing a system's performance under increasing levels of workload or user traffic to identify its capacity limits and potential bottlenecks. This method helps ensure that the system can handle growth and maintain a high level of performance.

Tip

Use realistic test data and scenarios that closely mimic real-world usage patterns to ensure accurate scalability assessment.

 83% of businesses say that scalability is a key factor in their long-term success. (Source: Deloitte)

Scalability Testing

How the method is applied

1. **Define Scalability Metrics:** Identify the key performance metrics to measure, such as response time, throughput, and resource utilization.

2. **Create Test Scenarios:** Develop test scenarios that simulate increasing levels of workload or user traffic.

3. **Set Up Test Environment:** Configure the test environment to closely resemble the production environment.

4. **Execute Tests:** Run the scalability tests and monitor the system's performance under different load levels.

5. **Analyze Results:** Evaluate the test results to identify the system's scalability limits and potential bottlenecks.

6. **Optimize and Retest:** Implement optimizations to address identified issues and retest to validate the improvements.

 Netflix conducts extensive scalability testing to ensure that their streaming platform can handle millions of concurrent users without compromising video quality or performance.

Design for Performance

How might we

Optimize our designs for speed, efficiency, and reliability, ensuring a seamless and responsive user experience?

What you can do with the method...

Design for Performance involves optimizing system design and architecture to ensure efficient resource utilization, fast response times, and scalability. This approach helps to deliver a smooth and responsive user experience, even under high load conditions.

Tip

Optimize database queries, minimize network latency, and implement caching mechanisms to improve system performance and responsiveness.

 A 1-second delay in page load time can result in a 7% reduction in conversions. (Source: Akamai)

Design for Performance

How the method is applied

1. **Performance Requirements:** Define clear performance requirements and goals for the system.

2. **Performance Modeling:** Create performance models to predict system behaviour and identify potential bottlenecks.

3. **Capacity Planning:** Plan for future growth and scalability by designing a system that can handle increasing workloads.

4. **Performance Optimization:** Optimize system components, such as databases, networks, and algorithms, to improve performance.

5. **Caching:** Implement caching mechanisms to reduce the load on backend systems and improve response times.

6. **Performance Testing:** Conduct regular performance testing to identify and address performance issues.

 Netflix heavily invests in designing for performance to ensure that its streaming service delivers a smooth and uninterrupted viewing experience to millions of users worldwide.

Design for Accessibility

How might we

create inclusive designs that are usable and accessible to people with diverse abilities, ensuring equal access to information and functionality?

What you can do with the method...

Designing for accessibility involves considering the needs of users with various disabilities, such as visual, auditory, motor, and cognitive impairments. By following accessibility guidelines and best practices, designers can create experiences that are usable and inclusive for all users.

Tip

Go beyond compliance with accessibility guidelines and strive to create inclusive experiences that empower users of all abilities.

 15% of the world's population, or over 1 billion people, live with some form of disability, making accessibility crucial. (Source: World Health Organization)

Design for Accessibility

How the method is applied

1. **Understand Accessibility Guidelines:** Familiarize yourself with accessibility guidelines, such as WCAG (Web Content Accessibility Guidelines), and how they apply to your design work.

2. **Consider Diverse User Needs:** Identify the range of disabilities and challenges users may face when interacting with your design.

3. **Provide Clear Structure and Navigation:** Use clear headings, labels, and landmarks to help users navigate and understand the content.

4. **Ensure Sufficient Contrast:** Use high-contrast color combinations to ensure readability for users with visual impairments.

5. **Offer Multiple Modes of Interaction:** Provide alternative ways to interact with the design, such as keyboard navigation and voice control.

 Government websites are required to follow strict accessibility guidelines to ensure that all citizens can access and use online services, regardless of their abilities or disabilities.

Design for Inclusivity

How might we

Design products and experiences that are accessible, usable, and welcoming to users of all backgrounds, abilities, and perspectives?

What you can do with the method...

Design for inclusiveness involves designing products and experiences that are accessible and usable by a wide range of users, regardless of their abilities, backgrounds, or perspectives. This method focuses on understanding and accommodating the diverse needs of users to create solutions that are equitable and inclusive.

Tip

Engage with diverse user groups throughout the design process to ensure that the solution meets the needs of a wide range of users.

 Inclusive design can increase market reach by up to 20%, making products accessible to a broader audience. (Source: Microsoft)

Design for Inclusivity

How the method is applied

1. **Understand User Diversity:** Conduct user research to identify the diverse needs, abilities, and perspectives of the target user group.

2. **Set Inclusivity Goals:** Define clear goals for inclusivity and accessibility in the design.

3. **Follow Inclusive Design Principles:** Apply inclusive design principles, such as flexibility, simplicity, and perceivability, throughout the design process.

4. **Design for Accessibility:** Ensure that the design meets accessibility standards and guidelines, such as WCAG.

5. **Test with Diverse Users:** Conduct user testing with a diverse range of users to validate the inclusivity and accessibility of the design.

6. **Continuously Improve:** Monitor user feedback and continuously improve the design to meet the evolving needs of diverse users.

 Microsoft's Xbox Adaptive Controller was designed with inclusivity in mind, providing a customizable gaming experience for players with limited mobility.

Design for User Engagement

How might we

Design products and experiences that capture and maintain user attention, encouraging regular interaction and long-term engagement?

What you can do with the method...

Design for User Engagement involves creating systems that capture and maintain user attention and interest over time. This approach focuses on providing value, motivation, and incentives for users to engage with the system regularly.

Tip

Use gamification techniques, such as rewards and challenges, to encourage user engagement and motivation.

 Engaged users are 4 times more likely to refer a product to others. (Source: Gallup)

Design for User Engagement

How the method is applied

1. **User Motivation:** Understand user motivations and design the system to align with them.

2. **Gamification:** Use gamification techniques, such as points, badges, and leaderboards, to encourage user engagement and motivation.

3. **Personalization:** Personalize the user experience based on user preferences, behaviors, and goals.

4. **Social Features:** Incorporate social features, such as sharing and collaboration, to encourage user engagement and interaction.

5. **Feedback and Rewards:** Provide feedback and rewards to users for their engagement and achievements.

6. **Analytics and Optimization:** Use analytics to track user engagement and optimize the system based on user behavior and feedback.

 Duolingo, a language learning app, uses gamification techniques such as points, streaks, and leaderboards to encourage users to engage with the app regularly and make learning fun and rewarding.

Design for User Retention

How might we

Create value, incentives, and experiences that encourage users to continue using our products over time?

What you can do with the method...

Design for User Retention involves creating systems that keep users engaged and motivated to continue using the system over time. This approach focuses on providing value, incentives, and reasons for users to return to the system regularly.

Tip

Provide personalized recommendations and content to keep users engaged and coming back to the system.

 Increasing customer retention rates by 5% can increase profits by 25% to 95%. (Source: Bain & Company)

Design for User Retention

How the method is applied

1. **Onboarding:** Design an effective onboarding process that helps users understand the value and benefits of the system.

2. **Value Proposition:** Clearly communicate the value proposition of the system and how it benefits users.

3. **Personalization:** Personalize the user experience based on user preferences, behaviors, and goals to keep them engaged.

4. **Notifications and Reminders:** Use notifications and reminders to keep users engaged and encourage them to return to the system.

5. **Loyalty Programs:** Implement loyalty programs and rewards to incentivize users to continue using the system over time.

6. **Customer Support:** Provide excellent customer support to address user issues and concerns and maintain user satisfaction.

 Amazon Prime uses a combination of personalized recommendations, free shipping, and exclusive content to retain users and encourage them to continue their subscription over time.

Design for User Acquisition

How might we

Design products and experiences that attract and acquire new users effectively, considering their needs, motivations, and behaviors?

What you can do with the method...

Design for User Acquisition involves creating systems that effectively attract and acquire new users. This approach focuses on optimizing the user journey from initial awareness to sign-up and onboarding.

Tip

Optimize the user registration and onboarding process to minimize friction and encourage user sign-ups.

 Companies that excel at user acquisition grow revenues 2.5 times faster than their peers. (Source: McKinsey)

Design for User Acquisition

How the method is applied

1. **User Personas:** Develop user personas to understand the needs, goals, and behaviors of potential users.

2. **Value Proposition:** Clearly communicate the value proposition of the system and how it benefits users.

3. **Landing Pages:** Design effective landing pages that communicate the value proposition and encourage user sign-ups.

4. **Call-to-Action:** Use clear and compelling calls-to-action to encourage users to sign up or try the system.

5. **Referral Programs:** Implement referral programs to encourage existing users to refer new users to the system.

6. **Advertising and Marketing:** Use targeted advertising and marketing campaigns to reach potential users and encourage them to try the system.

 Dropbox used a referral program that rewarded users with additional storage space for referring new users, which helped them acquire millions of new users quickly and cost-effectively.

Design for User Onboarding

How might we

Create onboarding experiences that help new users understand, explore, and derive value from our products quickly and easily?

What you can do with the method...

Design for User Onboarding involves creating an effective onboarding process that helps new users understand and start using the system quickly and easily. This approach focuses on guiding users through the key features and benefits of the system and helping them achieve their goals.

Tip

Use progressive disclosure to gradually introduce users to the features and functionality of the system, rather than overwhelming them all at once.

 Effective user onboarding can improve user retention rates by 50%. (Source: Wyzowl)

Design for User Onboarding

How the method is applied

1. **User Goals:** Identify the key goals and tasks that new users want to achieve with the system.

2. **Onboarding Flow:** Design an onboarding flow that guides users through the key features and benefits of the system.

3. **Progressive Disclosure:** Use progressive disclosure to gradually introduce users to the features and functionality of the system.

4. **Contextual Help:** Provide contextual help and guidance to users as they navigate the system.

5. **Feedback and Encouragement:** Provide feedback and encouragement to users as they complete key tasks and milestones.

6. **Analytics and Optimization:** Use analytics to track user behavior during onboarding and optimize the process based on user feedback and data.

 Slack, a team collaboration tool, uses a simple and intuitive onboarding process that guides new users through the key features and benefits of the system, helping them start collaborating with their team quickly and easily.

Design for User Feedback

How might we

Actively seek, analyze, and incorporate user feedback into our design process to continuously improve the user experience?

What you can do with the method...

Design for User Feedback involves creating systems that actively seek and incorporate user feedback to continuously improve the user experience. This approach focuses on gathering user insights and using them to make data-driven design decisions.

Tip

Use in-app feedback mechanisms, such as surveys and polls, to gather user feedback and insights directly within the system.

 Companies that actively seek and act on user feedback are 21% more profitable than those that don't. (Source: Gallup)

Design for User Feedback

How the method is applied

1. **Feedback Channels:** Provide multiple channels for users to provide feedback, such as in-app feedback, surveys, and user interviews.

2. **Feedback Prompts:** Use in-app prompts and notifications to encourage users to provide feedback at key moments in their journey.

3. **Feedback Analysis:** Analyze user feedback to identify common themes, issues, and opportunities for improvement.

4. **Prioritization:** Prioritize feedback based on impact and feasibility, and incorporate it into the design and development roadmap.

5. **Communication:** Communicate with users about how their feedback is being used to improve the system and the impact it has had.

6. **Continuous Improvement:** Use feedback as part of a continuous improvement process to iteratively enhance the user experience over time.

 Airbnb uses a combination of in-app feedback, surveys, and user interviews to gather insights from hosts and guests, which they use to continuously improve the user experience and address pain points.

Gamification

How might we

Incorporate game design elements and principles into our products and services to increase user engagement, motivation, and loyalty?

What you can do with the method...

Gamification involves applying game design elements, such as points, badges, leaderboards, and challenges, to non-game contexts to make tasks more engaging and rewarding. By tapping into users' intrinsic motivations, designers can create experiences that drive desired behaviors and outcomes.

Tip

Align gamification elements with users' intrinsic motivations and goals to create meaningful and engaging experiences.

 71% of employees report feeling more engaged when using gamification elements at work (Gartner)

Gamification

How the method is applied

1. **Identify Desired Behaviors:** Determine the key behaviors and actions you want to encourage through gamification.

2. **Understand User Motivations:** Research users' intrinsic motivations and what drives their engagement and participation.

3. **Select Relevant Game Elements:** Choose game elements that align with user motivations and the desired behaviors, such as points, badges, or challenges.

4. **Integrate into User Experience:** Seamlessly integrate gamification elements into the user experience, ensuring they enhance rather than disrupt the core functionality.

5. **Monitor and Adjust:** Continuously monitor user engagement and adjust the gamification strategy based on data and feedback.

 Duolingo, a language learning app, successfully uses gamification to keep users engaged and motivated. By incorporating elements like experience points, streaks, and leaderboards, Duolingo creates a sense of progress and achievement that encourages users to maintain their language learning habits.

Orchestrate and Align

This phase focuses on deep user understanding, uncovering insights, and building empathy through immersive research techniques.

1. Project Management
2. Stakeholder Management
3. Risk Analysis
4. ROI of UX Design
5. Negotiation Skills
6. Design Reviews
7. Design Sprints

Orchestrate and Align

Project Management

How might we

Plan, execute, and control design projects effectively to deliver high-quality results on time and within budget?

What you can do with the method…

Project management involves applying knowledge, skills, and techniques to execute projects effectively and efficiently. By planning, organizing, and managing resources, designers can ensure that projects are completed on time, within budget, and to the required quality standards.

Tip

Regularly communicate project status, risks, and changes to stakeholders to ensure transparency and alignment.

 Effective project management can increase project success rates by up to 67% (PMI)

Project Management

How the method is applied

1. **Define Project Scope:** Clearly define the project's goals, deliverables, and constraints to establish a shared understanding among stakeholders.

2. **Create a Project Plan:** Develop a comprehensive plan that includes tasks, timelines, milestones, and resource allocation.

3. **Manage Resources:** Allocate and manage resources, such as team members, budget, and tools, to ensure project success.

4. **Monitor Progress:** Regularly track and report on project progress, identifying and addressing any issues or risks that arise.

5. **Communicate and Collaborate:** Foster open communication and collaboration among team members and stakeholders to ensure alignment and resolve any conflicts.

 Adobe used project management techniques to successfully launch Adobe XD, their UX design and prototyping tool. By defining clear project goals, creating a detailed project plan, and regularly communicating with stakeholders, the Adobe XD team was able to deliver a high-quality product on time and within budget, despite the complexity and scale of the project.

Orchestrate and Align

Stakeholder Management

How might we

Effectively manage and align the needs and expectations of various stakeholders to ensure project success?

What you can do with the method...

Stakeholder management involves identifying, analyzing, and engaging with individuals or groups who have an interest in or influence on a project's success. By understanding stakeholder needs, designers can align project goals, communicate effectively, and ensure stakeholder satisfaction.

Tip

Regularly engage with stakeholders to understand their needs, concerns, and expectations, and keep them informed of project progress and decisions.

 Effective stakeholder management can reduce project risks by 30% (PwC)

Stakeholder Management

How the method is applied

1. **Identify Stakeholders:** Identify all individuals or groups who have an interest in or influence on the project, such as users, clients, developers, and business leaders.

2. **Analyze Stakeholder Needs:** Assess each stakeholder's needs, expectations, and potential impact on the project.

3. **Develop Engagement Strategies:** Create strategies for engaging with each stakeholder group, considering their level of influence and interest.

4. **Communicate Regularly:** Establish regular communication channels to keep stakeholders informed of project progress, decisions, and any issues that arise.

5. **Manage Expectations:** Proactively manage stakeholder expectations by clearly communicating project scope, timelines, and constraints.

 Salesforce manages stakeholder expectations in CRM development by engaging diverse stakeholders such as end-users, developers, and business leaders. Through needs analysis, user groups, and transparent communication, Salesforce ensures its platform stays innovative and user-focused, maintaining high customer satisfaction and loyalty.

Risk Analysis

How might we

Proactively identify, assess, and prioritize potential risks to minimize their impact on the project's success?

What you can do with the method...

Risk analysis involves identifying, assessing, and prioritizing potential risks that could impact a project's success. By proactively managing risks, designers can minimize their impact on the project's timeline, budget, and quality.

Tip

Prioritize risks based on their potential impact and likelihood, focusing on mitigating the most critical risks first.

 Proactive risk analysis can help identify and mitigate potential project issues, reducing project delays by 20% (Gartner)

Risk Analysis

How the method is applied

1. **Identify Risks:** Brainstorm potential risks that could impact the project, considering factors such as technology, resources, and stakeholders.

2. **Assess Risk Impact and Likelihood:** Evaluate each risk based on its potential impact on the project and the likelihood of it occurring.

3. **Prioritize Risks:** Prioritize risks based on their impact and likelihood, focusing on the most critical risks first.

4. **Develop Mitigation Strategies:** Create strategies to mitigate or avoid each risk, assigning responsibility and resources as needed.

5. **Monitor and Adjust:** Continuously monitor risks throughout the project, adjusting mitigation strategies as needed based on changing circumstances.

 During the development of a new mobile banking app, the UX design team conducted a risk analysis to identify potential usability and security risks. By assessing the impact and likelihood of each risk, the team was able to prioritize and mitigate the most critical risks, such as the potential for user error in transferring funds. This proactive approach helped ensure the app's successful launch and positive user reception.

Orchestrate and Align

ROI of UX Design

How might we

Demonstrate the business value of investing in UX design by measuring and communicating its impact on key metrics?

What you can do with the method…

Calculating the Return on Investment (ROI) of UX design involves measuring the financial and non-financial benefits of investing in UX, such as increased user satisfaction, reduced development costs, and improved conversion rates. By demonstrating the tangible value of UX design, designers can secure buy-in and resources from stakeholders.

Tip

Communicate the value of UX design in terms of business metrics, such as increased conversion rates, customer loyalty, and cost savings.

 Every $1 invested in UX design can return an average of $100 (Forrester Research)

ROI of UX Design

How the method is applied

1. **Identify Key Metrics:** Determine the key business metrics that UX design can impact, such as user engagement, conversion rates, and customer loyalty.

2. **Establish Baseline Measurements:** Measure the current state of the key metrics to establish a baseline for comparison.

3. **Implement UX Improvements:** Identify and implement UX design improvements that address user needs and pain points.

4. **Measure Impact:** Measure the impact of the UX improvements on the key metrics, comparing them against the baseline.

5. **Calculate ROI:** Calculate the ROI of the UX investment by comparing the benefits (e.g., increased revenue, cost savings) to the costs of implementation.

 An e-commerce company invested in a UX redesign of their checkout process, with the goal of reducing cart abandonment and increasing conversions. By measuring the impact of the redesign on key metrics, the company found that the improved UX resulted in a 20% increase in conversion rates and a 15% increase in average order value. This translated to a significant ROI for the UX investment, demonstrating the tangible value of UX design to the business.

Negotiation Skills

How might we

Use effective communication and collaboration techniques to align project goals, resources, and priorities with stakeholders?

What you can do with the method...

Negotiation skills enable designers to effectively communicate and collaborate with stakeholders, such as clients, developers, and business leaders. By finding common ground, building trust, and creating win-win solutions, designers can ensure that projects stay on track and meet the needs of all parties involved.

Tip

Practice active listening and seek to understand the other party's perspective and underlying interests to find mutually beneficial solutions.

 Strong negotiation skills can save companies an average of 11% on project costs (Harvard Business Review)

Negotiation Skills

How the method is applied

1. **Prepare and Set Goals:** Clearly define your goals and priorities before entering into a negotiation, and anticipate the other party's needs and concerns.

2. **Practice Active Listening:** Listen attentively to the other party, asking questions and summarizing their points to ensure understanding and demonstrate empathy.

3. **Find Common Ground:** Identify shared interests and goals to build trust and establish a foundation for collaboration.

4. **Generate Options:** Brainstorm potential solutions that address the needs and concerns of all parties involved.

5. **Seek Win-Win Outcomes:** Strive for mutually beneficial agreements that satisfy the key interests of all stakeholders.

 During the redesign of a major e-commerce website, the UX design team used negotiation skills to align the project's goals and priorities with the needs of various stakeholders. By actively listening to the concerns of the marketing, sales, and development teams, and finding common ground, the designers were able to create a solution that met the needs of all parties and ensured the project's success.

Design Reviews

How might we

Grasp the essence and process of design reviews for enhancing product quality and user experience.

What you can do with the method...

Design Reviews are structured evaluations of design work, ensuring alignment with goals and standards. They offer designers a platform to present their work, collect feedback, and refine based on insights. This tool helps teams spot inconsistencies, usability issues, and areas for improvement. It also fosters collaboration, ensuring that all stakeholders are aligned and designs are optimized for the target audience.

Tip

When conducting design reviews, focus on constructive feedback. It's crucial to differentiate between personal preferences and genuine usability concerns. Encourage a diverse group of participants, as this ensures a holistic review. Remember, the primary goal is to enhance the design, not to critique the designer.

 Regular design reviews can improve design quality by 25% by incorporating diverse perspectives and feedback. (Source: Nielsen Norman Group)

Design Reviews

How the method is applied

1. **Preparation:** Clearly define the scope of the review. Decide on the designs to be reviewed and gather relevant materials.

2. **Invite Participants:** Include a mix of designers, developers, stakeholders, and sometimes users, to gain a comprehensive perspective.

3. **Set Guidelines:** Start with a brief on the objective of the design and the context. Encourage feedback that's specific, actionable, and kind.

4. **Presentation:** The designer showcases the design, explaining their choices and the problems they're addressing.

5. **Feedback Collection:** Participants share their insights. It's essential to note both positive aspects and areas of improvement.

6. **Action Plan:** Post-review, compile the feedback, and prioritize changes. Determine the revisions needed and assign tasks for implementation.

 Uber conducts regular design reviews to ensure its products meet high standards of usability and visual design.

Orchestrate and Align

Design Sprints

How might we

Swiftly prototype and validate design ideas, maximizing efficiency and innovative output.

What you can do with the method...

Design Sprints are intensive five-day processes that transform ideas into prototypes, tested with real users. Originating from Google Ventures, it's a collaborative effort involving designers, stakeholders, and developers. The goal is to address critical business questions, swiftly iterate on design solutions, and gain user feedback. By the end, teams will have tangible designs and clarity on the project's direction.

Tip

Always set clear objectives for your sprint. Remember, it's not about perfecting the design but rapidly testing hypotheses to gain insights and make informed decisions.

 Design sprints can reduce project timelines by 50% by rapidly prototyping and testing ideas. (Source: Google Ventures)

Design Sprints

How the method is applied

1. **Understand (Day 1):** Define the problem and align the team. Discuss and identify the main challenge for the week.

2. **Sketch (Day 2):** Team members ideate independently, sketching potential solutions, fostering a wealth of diverse ideas.

3. **Decide (Day 3):** Converge on the best ideas. Vote and choose the most promising solutions to prototype.

4. **Prototype (Day 4):** Build a realistic, yet simple prototype. It should emulate the final product's look and feel.

5. **Test (Day 5):** Present the prototype to real users. Capture feedback and observe their interactions for insights.

6. **Reflect:** After testing, analyze findings. Determine next steps, whether it's iterating on the design or moving to development.

 Google has popularized the use of design sprints to rapidly prototype and test new ideas.

UX Design Blueprints

1. Contextual Inquiry
2. Ethnographic Studies
3. User Interviews
4. Persona Creation
5. User Journey Mapping
6. Competitive Analysis
7. Affinity Mapping
8. Task Analysis
9. Jobs To Be Done
10. Value Proposition Design
11. Business Model Canvas
12. Brainstorming
13. Lean UX
14. System Usability Scale
15. Time on Task Measurement
16. Component Library
17. Concept Mapping
18. Scenario Development
19. Rapid Prototyping
20. Usability Testing
21. A/B Testing

Download free printable blueprints (scan QR code)

Contextual Inquiry

Date: _____

Project Information:

Project Name: _____   Location Details: _____

Researcher(s): _____   Stakeholders: _____

Context & Tasks

Objective: _____

Participant Name	Demographics	Selection Criteria

Task Description	Task Questions	

Ethnographic Studies

Date:

Project Information:

Project Name: .... Location Details: ....

Researcher(s): .... Stakeholders: ....

Context & Tasks

Primary Goal: .... Secondary Goal: ....

Participant Name	Demographics	Selection Criteria
....	....	....
....	....	....

Fieldwork Plan	Observations	Findings
....	....	....
....	....	....

UX Mastery: Author – Mayur Chaudhary & Kishore Kankipati

User Interviews

Date:

Project Information:

Project Name:

Interviewer(s)   Stakeholders:

Objectives

Interview Guide

Participant Name	Demographics	Selection Criteria

Key Insights   Analysis

Persona Creation

Date:

Project Information:

Project Name:

Interviewer(s): Stakeholders:

User Data

Demographics

Age:

Gender:

Occupation:

Location:

Income:

Education:

Identified Patterns

Behavioral

Motivations

Pain Points

Validation Notes

User Feedback: Revisions:

UX Mastery: Author – Mayur Chaudhary & Kishore Kankipati

User Journey Mapping

Date:

Project Information:

Project Name: _____

Interviewer(s): _____

Stakeholders: _____

Scope Definition

Key Scenarios: _____

Journey Map

	Awareness	Consideration	Purchase	Onboarding	Retention
User Actions					
User Thoughts/ Emotions					
Pain Points					

Competitive Analysis

Date:

Project Information:

Project Name: .... Location Details: ....

Researcher(s): .... Stakeholders: ....

Competitor 1	Competitor 2	Competitor 3	Competitor 4
Criteria 1	Criteria 2	Criteria 3	Criteria 4
Strengths	Strengths	Strengths	Strengths
Weaknesses	Weaknesses	Weaknesses	Weaknesses
Features	Features	Features	Features

UX Mastery: Author - Mayur Chaudhary & Kishore Kankipati

Affinity Mapping

Date:

Project Information:

Project Name: Location Details:

Researcher(s):   Stakeholders:

Data Collection:

Source of Data   Collected Data

Group Name   Group Name

Description   Description

Notes   Notes

Theme Name   Theme Name

Description   Description

Notes   Notes

Task Analysis

Date:

Project Information:

Project Name: ....

Researcher(s): ....

Location Details: ....

Stakeholders: ....

Task Definition

Task Name ....

Objective ....

Frequency ....

Steps

Step 1: ....

Description ....
....
....

Step 2: ....

Description ....
....
....

Step 3: ....

Description ....
....
....

Issues Identified ....
....

Opportunities ....
....

UX Mastery: Author – Mayur Chaudhary & Kishore Kankipati

Value Proposition Design

Project Information:

Project Name: _____ Location Details: _____

Researcher(s): _____ Stakeholders: _____

User Needs

Need 1 _____

Need 2 _____

Need 3 _____

Need 4 _____

Need 5 _____

Statement: _____
_____

Features

Feature 1 _____

Feature 2 _____

Feature 3 _____

Feature 4 _____

Feature 5 _____

For [target customer] who [statement of need or opportunity], the [product/service name] is a [product category] that [statement of benefit]. Unlike [primary competitive alternative], our product [statement of primary differentiation].

Date: _____

Jobs to be Done

Date:

Project Information:

Project Name: .... Location Details: ....

Researcher(s): .... Stakeholders: ....

Job Identification

Job 1 .... Steps: ....

Job 2 .... Steps: ....

Job 3 .... Steps: ....

Job 4 .... Steps: ....

Prioritization

High Priority ....

Medium Priority ....

Low Priority ....

Job Statement

For ....

Who ....

Our Product ....

Provides: ....

Unlike ....

Our Product ....

UX Mastery: Author – Mayur Chaudhary & Kishore Kankipati

Business Model Canvas

Project Information:

Project Name: .... Facilitator(s): .... Date: ....

Stakeholders: ....

Key Partners	Key Activities	Value Propositions	Customer Relationships	Customer Segments
	Key Resources		Channels	

Cost Structure	Revenue Streams

Brainstorming

Date:

Project Information:

Project Name: _____

Facilitator(s): _____

Participants: _____

Stakeholders: _____

Problem Definition _____

Group Rules _____

Ideas

Evaluation

Idea 1 _____ ○ ○ ○

Idea 2 _____ ○ ○ ○

Idea 3 _____ ○ ○ ○

Idea 4 _____ ○ ○ ○

UX Mastery: Author – Mayur Chaudhary & Kishore Kankipati

Lean UX

Date:

Project Information:

Project Name: _____

Facilitator(s): _____

Stakeholders: _____

Hypothesis Statement:

Assumptions	Experiment	Results

Learnings

System Usability Scale

Date:

Project Information:

Project Name: _____

Researcher(s): _____   Stakeholders: _____

SUS Statements	Strongly Disagree	Disagree	Neutral	Agree	Strongly Agree
1. I think that I would like to use this system frequently.	1	2	3	4	5
2. I found the system unnecessarily complex.	1	2	3	4	5
3. I thought the system was easy to use.	1	2	3	4	5
4. I think that I would need the support of a technical person to be able to use this system.	1	2	3	4	5
5. I found the various functions in this system were well integrated.	1	2	3	4	5
6. I thought there was too much inconsistency in this system.	1	2	3	4	5
7. I would imagine that most people would learn to use this system very quickly.	1	2	3	4	5
8. I found the system very cumbersome to use.	1	2	3	4	5
9. I felt very confident using the system.	1	2	3	4	5
10. I needed to learn a lot of things before I could get going with this system.	1	2	3	4	5

UX Mastery: Author – Mayur Chaudhary & Kishore Kankipati

Time on Task Measurement

Date:

Project Information:

Project Name: _____

Researcher(s): _____ Stakeholders: _____

Task Description	Participant 1	Participant 2	Participant 3	Average Time
	Start Time	Start Time	Start Time	
	End Time	End Time	End Time	
	Elapsed Time	Elapsed Time	Elapsed Time	

Task Description	Participant 1	Participant 2	Participant 3	Average Time
	Start Time	Start Time	Start Time	
	End Time	End Time	End Time	
	Elapsed Time	Elapsed Time	Elapsed Time	

Recommendations:

Component Library

Project Information:

Project Name: _____

Designer: _____

Stakeholders: _____

Date: _____

Component Name	Usage	Attributes

Design Canvas

UX Mastery: Author – Mayur Chaudhary & Kishore Kankipati

Concept Mapping

Date:

Project Information:

Project Name:

Designer: Stakeholders:

Concept

	Description
Concept 1	
Concept 2	
Concept 3	

Theme

Description

Connections

From Concept	To Concept	Nature of Connection

Scenario Development

Date: _____

Project Information:

Project Name: _____

Designer: _____   Stakeholders: _____

Setting Stage

User Persona _____   Situation _____

Environment _____

Primary Goals _____   Task _____

Key Interactions

Touchpoints _____   User Actions _____   User Responses _____   Decisions _____

Challenges _____

Conclusion & Reflection Statement _____

UX Mastery: Author – Mayur Chaudhary & Kishore Kankipati

Feature Matrix

Date:

Project Information:

Project Name: _____

Designer: _____

Stakeholders: _____

Feature	Description	Current Design	Competitor A	Competitor B

Feature	Improvement Action	Timeline	Owner	

Prioritization Analysis

- High User Value / High Effort: Maybe
- High User Value / Low Effort: Yes
- Low User Value / High Effort: No
- Low User Value / Low Effort: Maybe

Axes: User Value (HIGH → LOW), Effort by Organization (HIGH → LOW)

Usability Testing Canvas

Project Information:

Project Name: _____   Location Details: _____

Researcher(s): _____   Stakeholders: _____

Date: _____

Task	Description	Observation	Issues Identified	Suggestions
Common Issues				

	Frequency	Severity	Recommendation

Common Issues	Improvement Action	Timeline	Owner

UX Mastery: Author – Mayur Chaudhary & Kishore Kankipati

A/B Testing

Date:

Project Information:

Project Name: _____

Designer: _____   Stakeholders: _____

Feature	Description	Version A	Version B

Metric	Description	Version A	Version B

Decision	Action	Timeline	Owner

References

Books:

- **The User Experience Team of One** by Leah Buley

- **Observing the User Experience: A Practitioner's Guide to User Research** by Elizabeth Goodman, Mike Kuniavsky, and Andrea Moed

- **The Lean Product Playbook: How to Innovate with Minimum Viable Products and Rapid Customer Feedback** by Dan Olsen

- **Creative Confidence: Unleashing the Creative Potential Within Us All** by Tom Kelley and David Kelley

- **Gamestorming: A Playbook for Innovators, Rulebreakers, and Changemakers** by Dave Gray, Sunni Brown, and James Macanufo

- **Sprint: How to Solve Big Problems and Test New Ideas in Just Five Days** by Jake Knapp, John Zeratsky, and Braden Kowitz

- **Prototyping: A Practitioner's Guide** by Todd Zaki Warfe

- **Design Leadership: How Top Design Leaders Build and Grow Successful Organizations** by Richard Banfield, Martin Ringlein, and Nate Walkingshaw

- **The Design Sprint: A Practical Guidebook for Building Great Digital Products** by Richard Banfield, C. Todd Lombardo, and Trace Wax

- **Design Systems** by Alla Kholmatova
- **Lean UX: Designing Great Products with Agile Teams** by Jeff Gothelf and Josh Seiden
- **Rocket Surgery Made Easy: The Do-It-Yourself Guide to Finding and Fixing Usability Problems** by Steve Krug
- **UX Playbook** by Mayur Chaudhary and Kishore Kankipati

Index

A
1. A/B Testing.....110
2. Affinity Mapping.....26
3. Agile Development.....146
4. AI-led Personalized Experiences...164
5. Analytics Monitoring.....132
6. Animation Timing.....84

B
7. Brainstorming.....46
8. Business Model Canvas.....32

C
9. Churn Rate Analysis.....168
10. Clickable Prototypes.....80
11. Cognitive Walkthrough.....120
12. Cohort Analysis.....170
13. Color Theory.....86
14. Component Library.....158
15. Competitive Analysis.....20
16. Concept Mapping.....48
17. Contextual Inquiry.....2
18. Conversion Funnel Analysis.....172
19. Customer Satisfaction Score..134

D
20. Design for Accessibility.....198
21. Design for Inclusivity.....200
22. Design for Performance.....196
23. Design for Scalability.....190
24. Design for Security.....192
25. Design for User Acquisition.....206
26. Design for User Engagement.202
27. Design for User Feedback.....210
28. Design for User Onboarding.....208
29. Design for User Retention.....205
30. Design Handoff.....156
31. Design Reviews.....226
32. Design Sprints.....228
33. Design System.....104
34. Design Thinking.....60
35. Design Tokens.....88
36. DevOps Pipeline Integration.....148
37. Diary Studies.....4

E
38. Empathy Mapping.....10
39. Error Rate Measurement.....142
40. Ethnographic Studies.....6
41. Eye Tracking.....128

F
42. Feature Matrix.....34
43. Feedback Surveys.....174
44. Field Survey.....176

G
45. Gap Analysis.....36
46. Gamification.....212
47. Grid Systems.....90
48. Guerrilla Testing.....112

H

49. Heuristic Evaluation.....118
50. High-fidelity Prototyping.....78

I

51. Iconography.....92
52. In-person Observations.....124
53. Interactive Wireframes.....76
54. Iterative Testing.....178

J

55. Jobs To Be Done.....28

K

56. Kano Model.....38

L

57. Lean UX.....62
58. Lifetime Value Analysis.....180
59. Longitudinal Study.....182
60. Low-fidelity Prototyping.....74

M

61. Micro-interactions.....94
62. Mind Mapping.....50
63. MoSCoW Method.....40
64. Mood Boards.....96

N

65. Negotiation Skills.....224
66. Net Promoter Score.....136

P

67. Pair Designing.....150
68. Paper Prototyping.....72
69. Participatory Design.....66
70. Performance Metrics.....184
71. Persona Creation.....12
72. Predictive User Feedback.....166
73. Project Management.....216

Q

74. QA Testing.....160

R

75. Rapid Prototyping.....70
76. Remote Usability Tests.....126
77. Requirement Prioritization.....42
78. Responsive Design Testing.....116
79. Risk Analysis.....220
80. ROI of UX Design.....222

S

81. Scalability Testing.....194
82. Scenario Development.....56
83. Service Design.....64
84. Sketching.....52
85. Six Thinking Hats.....58
86. Stakeholder Interviews.....14
87. Stakeholder Management.....218
88. Storyboarding.....54
89. Style Guide Development.....98
90. SWOT Analysis.....18
91. System Usability Scale.....138

T

92. Task Analysis.....26
93. Time-on-task Measurement.....140
94. Typography Studies.....100

U

95. Usability Checklist.....122
96. Usability Testing.....108
97. User Acceptance Testing (UAT).....152
98. User Analytics.....186
99. User Interviews.....8
100. User Journey Mapping.....16

V

101. Value Proposition Design.....30
102. Version Control.....154
103. Visual Hierarchy.....102
104. Visual Language & Brand Study.....82

W

105. Wizard of Oz Testing.....114

A book is a dream that you hold in your hand.

Thank you for holding this dream with us. We would love to hear your thoughts – feel free to reach out and connect!

Thank You!

Mayur Chaudhary
linkedin/ Instagram @**mayurchaudhary**

Kishore Kankipati
linkedin @**kankipati**

www.ingramcontent.com/pod-product-compliance
Lightning Source LLC
LaVergne TN
LVHW061608070526
838199LV00078B/7216